Field Linguistics

Field Linguistics
A Beginner's Guide

Terry Crowley

Edited and prepared for publication by
Nick Thieberger

OXFORD
UNIVERSITY PRESS

OXFORD

UNIVERSITY PRESS

Great Clarendon Street, Oxford OX2 6DP

Oxford University Press is a department of the University of Oxford.
It furthers the University's objective of excellence in research, scholarship,
and education by publishing worldwide in

Oxford New York

Auckland Cape Town Dar es Salaam Hong Kong Karachi
Kuala Lumpur Madrid Melbourne Mexico City Nairobi
New Delhi Shanghai Taipei Toronto

With offices in

Argentina Austria Brazil Chile Czech Republic France Greece
Guatemala Hungary Italy Japan Poland Portugal Singapore
South Korea Switzerland Thailand Turkey Ukraine Vietnam

Oxford is a registered trade mark of Oxford University Press
in the UK and in certain other countries

Published in the United States
by Oxford University Press Inc., New York

British Library Cataloguing in Publication Data

Data available

Library of Congress Cataloguing in Publication Data

Data available

Typeset by SPI Publisher Services, Pondicherry, India
Printed in Great Britain
on acid-free paper by
Biddles Ltd, www.biddles.co.uk

ISBN   978-019-928434-4 (hbk.)
ISBN   978-019-921370-2 (pbk.)

1 3 5 7 9 10 8 6 4 2

Contents

Preface

A huge number of the world's languages remain poorly described, or even completely undescribed. Many may have disappeared altogether by the end of the twenty-first century, and only a small number of people are doing anything about this. Even among linguists—who we might expect to be among the most concerned—there are surprisingly many who are doing surprisingly little.

This book deals with one aspect of the issue of linguistic diversity in the world: the task of linguistic documentation arising out of original research in the field. Although many linguistics programmes include a field methods component, I have often been asked by academics, 'When you do fieldwork, how do you actually start?' This suggests that researchers are possibly sometimes still being thrown into the field at the deep end, much as I suppose I was back in the early 1970s when I was sent on my first fieldtrip. I went with an abundance of enthusiasm, tempered with some trepidation, but not a whole lot of practical training. There therefore has to be a substantial need for a book such as this.

I have chosen to concentrate in this volume on only a subset of fieldwork activities. Clearly, somebody who is involved in recording a corpus of some variety of non-standard spoken English is just as much engaged in fieldwork as somebody who journeys forth to the Kamchatka Peninsula to document a previously undescribed language. While some of the issues are the same for all kinds of linguistic field research, the linguist who is heading for Kamchatka is likely to be faced with quite different sorts of issues from the linguist who is headed for the Bronx. The latter kind of field linguist is extremely well served with information about how to assemble a corpus (e.g. Milroy 1987), while the Kamchatka-bound linguist is much less well served.

There are, admittedly, other guides to linguistic fieldwork, but none seems to me to be completely satisfactory. Some were written in a different technological era when reel-to-reel tapes and typewriters were our main tools. Some are far too dry, concentrating on how to take notes and how to make satisfactory voice recordings, while ignoring the interrelationships between the linguist and language speakers as people. Some concentrate exclusively on problems arising from personal relationships in the field while sidestepping crucial issues of data-gathering. Some completely ignore the fact that fieldwork involves an array of ethical issues which need to be addressed, and treat fieldwork instead entirely as an exercise in advanced linguistic analysis. Some seem better designed for the experienced fieldworker who wants to look back on fieldwork, rather than being geared towards the neophyte who has yet to test the waters.

This volume is geared towards people who already have some background in linguistics and who intend to apply their training to the recording, analysis, and description of previously undescribed, or poorly described, languages. I anticipate that my major audience will be students enrolled in undergraduate courses in Field Methods (or any number of other courses with vaguely similar-sounding names), as well as graduate students—or even linguists occupying academic positions in universities—who are contemplating the possibility of their first foray into The Field.

However, I hope that this volume is appreciated also by anthropological fieldworkers, and those from kindred disciplines such as psychology, education, and sociology. There has long been a tradition of discussing, debating, and dissecting the process of fieldwork in the discipline of anthropology, and there are plenty of published sources dealing with a wide range of issues. However, this volume will offer a very different perspective.

I hold to the belief that real ethnographic insights cannot come only via questionnaires mediated by a hired translator. Even if a scholar is able to conduct interviews in the field in person through the medium of a lingua franca, he or she is still likely to be missing something that can only come through the local language. An ethnographer needs to be able to participate as well as to observe, and that means at the very least being able to understand something of what is being said in the immediate surroundings. While there is no pill that I can offer to instantaneously give you a command of a new language, I hope that this volume will at least make you understand that learning something of the language of your chosen field site is not only possible, but desirable, even essential.

I plan to avoid dryness by basing this account of linguistic fieldwork substantially on my own continuous career of fieldwork dating back to the early 1970s, as well as on what I know of the field experiences of some of my colleagues in linguistics. We all learn by our mistakes, and I have plenty of my own to share with you. I have also been observing the

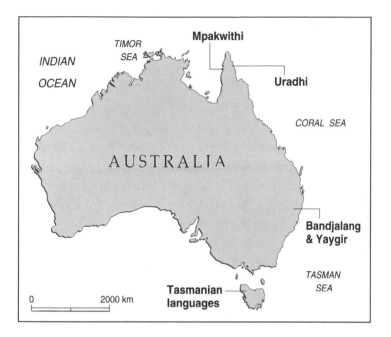

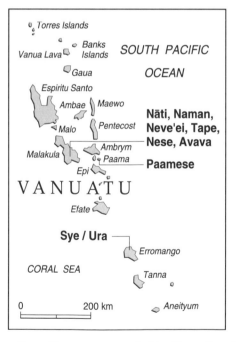

Location of languages recorded by Terry Crowley

failures of others for as long as I have been committing errors of my own, and some of these also provide excellent lessons for us all. (I promise to be discreet by not mentioning names.)

For those who do not know me, I should probably establish my credentials at the outset. I have produced—or am currently working on—published accounts ranging from very brief grammatical sketches to detailed grammatical accounts and accompanying dictionaries and collections of texts for eighteen different languages: Yaygir and Bandja-lang (northern New South Wales); Uradhi, Mpakwithi, and Cape York Creole (far north Queensland); Tasmanian (actually a number of lan-guages); Bislama (Vanuatu); Sye and Ura (Erromango, in Vanuatu); Paamese (Paama, in Vanuatu); Nāti, Naman, Neve'ei, Tape, Nese, and Avava (Malakula, in Vanuatu); Mwotlap (Banks Islands, in Vanuatu); and Gela (in Solomon Islands). In addition to English, I speak Bislama (and closely related Tok Pisin), Paamese, and French (but in reality, only with somebody who can't speak much English). In the past I have also been able to get by sufficiently well in Bahasa Indonesian, German, and Dutch to convince my examiners to give me surprisingly good passing grades. I have also taught linguistics at university level in both Papua New Guinea and Vanuatu for a total of twelve years, prior to taking up my current teaching position in New Zealand. I therefore consider myself, linguistically speaking, to have been around.

Terry Crowley

Hamilton (New Zealand)
April 2004

Acknowledgements

While I would like to claim the original title of this volume as my own creation, I must be honest and express my intellectual debt in this respect to Don Laycock. Don was a field linguist of considerable standing, having worked on a number of non-Austronesian languages in Papua New Guinea. He had long hankered after an excuse to write a book with the title *The Cunning Linguist* which was this book's working title. It was Don who originally encouraged me to pursue my interest in linguistics when I was only 15 years old and it is hard to find a way to thank him for this. Regrettably, Don died in 1988 and was never able to write his book. I dedicate this volume to his memory.

While I have based this volume substantially on my own experiences in the field, as well as my observations of other people in the field, I have also benefited from anecdotes, information, and advice from a number of people. I would like to offer my gratitude to the following for their contributions: Lyle Campbell, Michael Goldsmith, John Lynch, Bob Tonkinson, and Nick Thieberger.

Terry Crowley

Editor's Foreword

Terry Crowley's death in early 2005 left behind a number of works in progress, including the present book. I received the manuscript when it had already been read by two anonymous reviewers, and Terry had responded but not yet included their comments in the draft. He had sent me the manuscript for my input, especially on new technologies and fieldwork, and I have added that here. I have also added some references to further reading, taken account of the reviewers' comments, and updated some sections. Thanks to Eva Fenwick for work on the index, and to Margaret Florey and Marianne Mithun for their comments on an earlier draft.

Nicholas Thieberger

Publisher's Note

The publishers wish to express their gratitude to Dr Nicholas Thieberger for his work on finalizing the manuscript of this book which Professor Crowley had completed before his death on 15 January 2005.

1

Field Linguistics: Why Bother?

1.1 The threat to diversity

No linguist can fail to be aware that during the twentieth century a substantial number of small languages ceased to be spoken. Some of these were described before their last words were spoken; others were not. A substantial number of other speech traditions are now similarly destined for linguistic oblivion. We can hope social, economic, and political practices will be able to adapt such that the world's surviving linguistic diversity can survive. But if it cannot, then hopefully those languages that do disappear in the future will at least be recorded for posterity.

1.1.1 Some lessons from Truganini

Many of my readers have possibly never have heard of Truganini. Some of you may have heard of her, but you may know little of her life. But I want to begin this volume by asking, 'What could Truganini have taught us?'

So, who was Truganini then? In one sense, she was nobody terribly important at all. She was a woman who died in her sixties in 1876 in what was then something close to the end of the world, in the small British colonial settlement of Hobart, Tasmania. She was not formally educated at a time when there were many uneducated women. She never held any public office; she did not become a famous leader; and she never accumulated even a modicum of wealth. Although she had married, her husband died many years before her, and they produced no heirs. She wrote no books, and she is not credited with having expressed any great wisdom. Yet Truganini's life, and her death, was a great tragedy for us all.

For Truganini was the last person in the world to die who had grown up speaking one of the several Aboriginal languages of Tasmania. She was born shortly after the first European settlement at what is now Hobart in 1803. Her birthplace was some distance away from this settlement in what is still today pretty much a rural backwater. During the childhood that she spent with her people, while there were plenty of opportunities for contacts with European sealers and sawyers, she would have spoken with her parents and other close relatives in the language that today we call South-Eastern Tasmanian. Unfortunately, we have no way of knowing what Truganini's people called their own language, as nobody at the time ever seems to have thought to ask anybody this question.

Truganini was an observer of, and active participant in, events which can only be described as one of the great tragedies of colonial history in the nineteenth century (Ryan 1996). Truganini's own local people, as well as Tasmanian Aborigines all over the island, were disinherited of their lands, rivers, and seas and the bounteous resources that they provided them, as European settlers—some might prefer to see me use the term 'invaders'—rapidly fanned out from the new settlement of Hobart to establish farms, homesteads, and rural townships.

The Aboriginal population dropped very quickly, for a variety of reasons. European settlers brought with them a number of diseases to which they had for generations—if not centuries—enjoyed a degree of immunity. While among Europeans these diseases were not necessarily fatal, they produced high mortality rates among Aborigines when they were exposed to them for the first time. Aboriginal people's immunity was perhaps compromised anyway by lack of adequate nutrition brought about by restricted access to traditional hunting grounds when their land had been 'settled' by Europeans for pastoral purposes. To compound problems for the Aboriginal population, birth rates dropped as Aboriginal women were infected with the venereal diseases that were introduced by Europeans.

These factors alone would possibly have been enough ultimately to bring about a demographic catastrophe for Truganini's people. However, their problems were made worse by the brutal policy of the colonial government, which deliberately set about capturing every living Tasmanian Aborigine and relocating them to a previously unoccupied offshore island to which none of those people 'belonged'. This policy of ethnic separation—perhaps we should call this early apartheid or ethnic cleansing—and the establishment of the island 'homeland' was triggered by a period of active resistance by Aboriginal people along the expanding frontier of European settlement in which uncertain numbers of Europeans and Aborigines were killed in a series of violent skirmishes.

Once relocated, the surviving Aboriginal remnant population—which included Truganini—continued to decline in numbers. Their new home had an unhealthy climate, and the health care that was made available there was wholly inadequate. Eventually, this remote island settlement had to be abandoned and a new settlement was established for those who had survived at a healthier site closer to Hobart. However, the population had by this time passed the stage where it could be self-sustaining. The remaining members of this small community were past child-bearing age, and they died, one by one. The last to go was Truganini.

Before 1803, everybody in Tasmania spoke a Tasmanian Aboriginal language. After 1876, nobody did. Most of this tragedy played out during Truganini's lifetime.

There are many more tragedies that I could have reported along the way in the life of Truganini (Rae-Ellis 1981, 1988). One of these tragedies is the emergence of the myth that Truganini was the 'last Tasmanian', and with her passing, her race became 'extinct'. While she had no children of her own, many other Aboriginal women at the time did in fact bear children, albeit to European fathers working in the sealing trade.

Descendants of those children number several thousands in Tasmania today, and they proudly identify with their Aboriginal forebears. They now call themselves the Palawa people, after the documented word in one of the dozen or so original Palawa languages for '(Aboriginal) person'. Those children who originally grew up with their Aboriginal mothers and their sealer European fathers grew up speaking English. Some did learn a few words and set expressions in their mothers' languages, and some of these were passed down the generations to the present (Crowley 1993). However, those children did not learn how to construct new sentences in any of their mothers' languages, and they were able to carry on conversations only in English.

So, the Palawa population of Tasmania today is an English-speaking community, as it has been for generations. However, Palawa people have a proud association with their traditional past as well as a very powerful association with their tragic colonial history. They feel an overpowering sense of sadness over the loss of their ancestral languages. This sense of loss is all the harder to bear because so little of those languages was ever recorded.

Although today's Palawa people can trace their ancestry directly back to the Aboriginal women of the nineteenth century, many have so much European blood that physical appearance is no longer a reliable guide to ethnic identification. In such situations, having a language of your own that is clearly different from that of the English-speaking mainstream in today's overwhelmingly Anglo-Celtic Tasmania would be a powerful symbol of ethnic distinctness. The Welsh, for example, cannot be physically distinguished from their English neighbours, but anybody who has been to Wales and seen the street signs in Welsh and watched TV broadcasts in Welsh—and heard Welsh spoken in the local store—will be well aware of how important it is for Welsh people that the language should continue to be spoken.

But this is not what we find today among the Palawa people. While something of the original Tasmanian languages was recorded in the nineteenth century at a time when some of their last speakers were still alive, the records were extremely fragmentary. For one thing, Truganini's language was only one of possibly as many as a dozen separate languages, and some of the surviving records have mixed words up from different people as if there was just a single language.

In any case, words were written without the benefit of any kind of phonetic training. Observers simply recorded words using the spelling system of English. This is poorly enough designed for representing the sounds of English, and it is completely inadequate clearly to indicate the pronunciations of words in completely unknown languages. Finally, what was recorded of the Tasmanian languages was for the most part just words, with no recognition of the fact that in order properly to document a language, it is necessary also to show how these words are used in a wide range of different kinds of sentences. This means that we have almost no idea about how the grammars of these various languages were organized, and we will never be in a position to know this.

This, then, is the linguistic tragedy for today's Palawa people. In the face of repeated claims that they no longer exist as a distinct people, attempts are now being made to use Palawa words that were recorded in the nineteenth century to create a new language. They call this Palawa Kani, using the documented word *kani* meaning 'talk'. Of course, while a historically legitimate vocabulary can be reconstructed to some extent, with so little of the original grammar ever having been recorded, there are real limitations on what can be achieved with this kind of linguistic reconstitution, which nevertheless clearly has importance for Palawa people today.

1.1.2 The value of records

It didn't have to be this way, of course. If only a selection of different kinds of sentences had been accurately recorded by those nineteenth-century observers, we would be able to say so much more about the original grammatical patterns of these languages. There are places in the world where the original languages have become extinct, but enough information was left behind in written form that people today have been able to work out in a fair amount of detail what the original language was like. Today's Cornish language enthusiasts, for example, are able to make use of extensive written records that were kept before the last native speaker of the language died in 1777. If Truganini and her friends and relatives in that dwindling community had been given the education and the motivation, they could have written to each other in their languages, much as speakers of Cornish did in the 1700s. Alternatively, if a person with real linguistic insight had been able to sit down with Truganini to record her language in writing for posterity before she died, today's Palawa people could have been so much richer, for so little effort.

But the tragedy of Truganini's passing has become a tragedy not just for today's Palawa people. It is also a tragedy for humanity at large. This means that it is a tragedy for you, and for me, because with the loss of *any* language without documentation there is a whole range of questions that can never be answered.

For one thing, the records of the Tasmanian languages are so poor that it is impossible to say what their closest linguistic relatives might be. We might expect that they would be related to the Aboriginal languages of the Australian mainland. So might they have been, but the speakers of those languages had been cut off from the mainland by rising sea levels that came with the end of the last ice age about ten thousand years ago, the languages therefore had so long to evolve independently that any original similarities could easily have been obscured beyond recognition, even if we had excellent records. After all, the island of New Guinea has been cut off from mainland Australia for about the same length of time and the languages there show no convincing evidence of any kind of relationship with any of the Australian languages, or sometimes, even with each other.

However, having poor records has not stopped people from trying to make all manner of claims about historical connections between the original Tasmanians and other peoples. Some such claims are demonstrably wrong. For example, the claim that the Moriori of the Chatham Islands in New Zealand were a Tasmanoid people who were driven to extinction with the later arrival of the Maori people (King 2003: 56–7) can easily be shown to be wrong. Nineteenth-century documentation of the now-extinct Moriori language indicates very clearly that it was a close relative of Maori.

Others have claimed that the Tasmanian languages are related to the little-known languages of the Andaman Islanders as part of Greenberg's (1971) Indo-Pacific Hypothesis. No convincing proof of any kind of relationship between Tasmanian languages and any other language grouping has been, or can be, presented. However, the fact that such claims have been made at all seems to be encouraged—rather than discouraged—by the poor records of the Tasmanian languages.

But linguists ask questions about more than just linguistic history. The prime motivation in modern linguistics is to answer the question: What is possible in human language and what is not? If someone were to set out to design a language for Klingons—a rather violent non-human species whose name will be immediately recognizable to *Star Trek* aficionados—what features would they ascribe to it? It would obviously need to have plenty of vocabulary to express fighting and honour, such as *qaD* 'challenge', *bIj* 'punishment', *vaj* 'warrior', and *vID* 'be belligerent' (Okrand 1992: 181–5). But its grammar would probably also contain features that are never found at all in human languages, or which, if they are found, are very uncommon. So, while human languages very commonly have Subject Verb Object (SVO), Subject Object Verb (SOV), and Verb Subject Object (VSO) word orders, it is much less common for languages to have word orders in which objects come before subjects. The rarest word order in the world is Object Subject Verb (OSV), which is found in just a handful of languages. So, OVS would be a good candidate for Klingon syntax, if we wanted to make Klingon look as exotic as possible. Thus:

puq   *legh*   *yaS*
child   sees   officer
'The officer sees the child.' (Okrand 1992: 59)

So, what sorts of features *can* be present in human languages and what *cannot*? If I were able to talk to Truganini—and assuming that she might have been willing to share this kind of information with me—what kinds of questions might I have asked her? Of course, I would have wanted to know what the basic constituent order in her sentences was. Statistically, it is likely to have been SVO or SOV, but it could logically have been any of four other possibilities (VSO, VOS, OVS, OSV). There is one final possibility: it could also have been a language with free constituent order, as long as there were sufficient mechanisms elsewhere in the language for distinguishing between performers and undergoers of actions. If Truganini's language were of this 'non-configurational' type, we would therefore expect it to have had case markers of some kind: suffixes or prefixes, or postpositions or prepositions.

But I would want to find out so much more than just this. Among many other things, I would want to know if her language had a system of noun classes or not. If it did, I would want to know how many classes it had. I would want to know the details of the semantic content of each of these noun classes. I would want to know if the language marked a distinction between singular and plural nouns and, if it did, whether it made the same noun class distinctions with plural nouns as it did with singular nouns.

There are lots of languages where the number of noun classes is the same in the singular and plural. For instance, the definite article in Spanish in the singular is *el* with masculine nouns and *la* with feminine nouns, while with masculine plural nouns it is *los* and with feminine plural nouns it is *las*. There are also lots of languages in which more noun classes are marked with singular nouns than in the plural. For instance, there are separate definite articles in French for masculine singular nouns (*le*) and feminine singular nouns (*la*), but there is only a single article in the plural for nouns of both genders (*les*).

Predictions have been made that there are no languages in which the reverse is true, where there are more noun class distinctions marked with plural nouns than with singular nouns (Greenberg 1966: 95). So, if Truganini's language turned out to have noun classes, one of the things I would want to check is how its singular nouns behaved in relation to its plural nouns. If Truganini's language turned out to be the one and only language on earth which went against the prediction, she would have been able to teach us a valuable lesson, and Greenberg's earlier generalization would have to be revised.

Regrettably, the main lesson that Truganini can teach linguists now is the folly of allowing a language to disappear without properly documenting it first.

1.1.3 Diversity still undocumented

Tragic as the circumstances are surrounding the loss of Truganini's language, the situation that I have described is far from unique. Hers was one of perhaps a dozen distinct languages that were originally spoken in Tasmania, and we are left with only very fragmentary records of all of them. On the Australian mainland, none of the languages of Victoria has been spoken for many generations. Although some of these languages were rather better recorded thanks to the work of one linguist (Hercus 1969), none has been described in any great detail, and some have disappeared with only very fragmentary records. The last fluent speakers of a handful of languages in New South Wales were recorded in some detail by linguists who conducted fieldwork in the 1970s (Crowley 1978, Eades 1979, Donaldson 1980, Williams 1980), but most of the remaining languages disappeared with rather less complete records, or even records that can only be described as extremely fragmentary. It was estimated in 2001 that of the 250 or so languages that were originally spoken in Australia, only about 17 could be considered strong (McConvell and Thieberger 2001: 61).

Descriptions similar to what I have just recounted for parts of Australia can be repeated for many other parts of the world that have been subject to European colonial expansion in the last few centuries. While indigenous languages survive in some parts of the Americas—most notably in Central America and Amazonia—there are other parts of North and South America where there has been widespread language loss. In the United States, many of the original languages have disappeared (Nettle and Romaine 2000: 5), and this pattern is mirrored in much of Canada (Nettle and Romaine 2000: 8). Of course, the indigenous languages of the Caribbean have long been completely extinct, given that this was the first part of the New World to be settled after the arrival of Christopher Columbus (Crystal 2000: 24).

Tragic as these kinds of stories are, a volume such as this cannot devote too much time to crying over linguistic spilt milk. What has happened has happened and we cannot turn back the clock. What we need to do now is try to stop any more milk from being spilt. And there is quite a lot of milk in containers that are now teetering.

Of the remaining ninety languages in Australia which still have speakers, only twenty are currently being passed on to today's generation of children (McConvell and Thieberger 2001: 17), and there is no guarantee that they will all be in a position to pass on these languages in due course to their own children. There are substantial numbers of languages in North America that are probably now in their final generations of speakers. There are pressures in many other parts of the world from large languages on small languages which also have uncertain futures. One recent estimate has suggested that as few as 10 per cent of the world's 6,000 or so languages that are spoken today will continue to be spoken by the end of this century. While this is one of the more alarming among a wide range of predictions, if this turns out to be correct, then Truganini's tragedy stands to be played out at the rate of four or five languages a month, every year, for the whole century. Even if we experience a slower rate of extinction, then Truganini's tragedy may play out at only two or three languages a month (Krauss 1992: 6–7).

Let's think about this. We are not dealing with just idle statistics here, as real people and real communities are also involved. In the 1970s, I visited parts of northern New South Wales and far north Queensland to record people who were regarded at the time as the last speakers of the Bandjalang, Yaygir, Mpakwithi, and Uradhi languages. Since then, the people whose speech became the basis for published accounts of those languages (Crowley 1978, 1979, 1981, 1983) have all died. Since then, these written accounts have been used by subsequent generations in a variety of ways, including language learning lessons, and as support for applications for land rights for which it is necessary in Australian law to demonstrate an ancestral connection with the land in question.

While it is certainly more urgent for dying languages to be documented than it is to document those which continue to be passed on to succeeding generations of children, linguistic fieldwork does not have benefits just for speakers of dying languages. The bulk of the world's 6,000 or so languages are in fact still being passed on to children, though the pressures on many of these are such that we cannot expect that all will survive in the longer term.

The task of *fully* documenting even a single language is enormous. In fact, *no* language—not even English—has ever been truly *fully* described. (If it had, presumably we would be able to engage in person-to-computer chat sessions about Chomsky's politics, the Sapir–Whorf Hypothesis, and the likelihood that it will rain this afternoon.) Even if we were to lower our expectations somewhat, there is still a huge task of linguistic documentation awaiting us. For the sake of argument, let us assume that a language can be said to be reasonably 'well described' if there is a published grammar which runs to 200–300 pages of published text, since this approximates to what is expected of a doctoral dissertation. (Mind you, so limited would such an account be that a computer which had been programmed with this grammar would still probably make for a very strange conversationalist.) Of course, for a language to be considered to be truly 'well described', there should also be a published dictionary of roughly similar length which would be a reasonable reflection of the everyday vocabulary.

Anything less than this should qualify a language as being less than 'well described'. So, a language for which there is only a published grammar, or only a published dictionary, cannot yet be considered to be adequately described. A language with a grammatical description and dictionary that each run to between 100 and 200 pages could perhaps be considered to be only moderately well described, while a description of less than this could be considered as representing only a sketchy account.

While the world's major languages no doubt meet these fairly basic criteria for being well described, the descriptive coverage of the world's many small languages—which are, of course, also those which are most vulnerable to language shift—is much more patchy. I would like to be able to report how many of the total number of the world's languages remain undescribed or only sketchily described, but I do not have these kinds of figures. Nor do I have any figures for how many of the world's languages can be regarded as moderately described.

However, let us look at one country with which I am quite familiar. Vanuatu is the world's most diverse nation in terms of the number of languages per head of population. Its 200,000 people speak at least 100 quite distinct languages. About twenty of these are in fact moribund and are destined to disappear with the passing of the current older generation, which leaves about eighty languages that are being actively passed on to younger generations. Of these, only two qualify as well described according to the criteria that I have just presented. The vast bulk of these languages—well over eighty in all—are either almost completely undescribed or only sketchily known (Lynch and Crowley 2001: 19).

I do not know how safe it would be to extrapolate from this situation to other parts of the world, but I do know that there are huge numbers of languages in the world that are only poorly described. Many of the world's linguistic hotspots—the rest of Melanesia, including Papua New Guinea, Indonesia, India, the Caucasus, equatorial Africa, Amazonia—are covered to extents that are probably not hugely different from what we currently find in Vanuatu. That is, for the many parts of the world, there is likely to be a scattering of well-described languages and a somewhat larger number of moderately-described languages, while a very large number of languages remain either completely unknown or only very sketchily known.

However, there are some rays of hope. In Australia in the 1960s, the situation would have been very similar to what I have just described for Vanuatu, but since the 1970s there have been huge strides in the documentation of those languages which are still spoken. Some of those languages that have only recently been documented have in fact in the meantime lost their final speakers. In these cases, Truganini's tragedy has not been repeated, at least not in its entirety.

1.2 The 'Big Questions'

Linguistics could not be linguistics without linguistic descriptions. If we are going to respond to the Big Questions of our science—how different can languages be? and how similar must different languages be?—our answers can only be as accurate as the extent of the raw data that we have looked at. Linguistics therefore depends crucially on the availability of a broad collection of detailed and accurate descriptions of the world's languages.

1.2.1 Armchairs and dirty feet

It could be said that there are two kinds of linguists in the world. Let me caricature each type with the labels 'armchair linguists' and 'dirty-feet linguists'.

Armchair linguists often publish quite extensively without necessarily putting in any effort to conduct original research on any language, except perhaps their own native language, which surprisingly often seems to be English. Some linguists argue that it is not really necessary to consider data from a wide range of languages when talking about 'language universals', as it is far more useful to analyse data from a restricted number of languages obtained from great 'derivational depth'. This corresponds to the tradition of the 'deep–narrow' approach to the study of linguistic diversity (Comrie 1981: 1–5). It is not difficult to conjure up an image of a linguist in this tradition relaxing in his or her comfy chair, conjuring up grammatical sentences, along with a set of contrasting ungrammatical strings of words which can be marked with asterisks, for inclusion in his or her next paper in *Linguistic Inquiry*.

The other kind of linguist is someone who gets actively involved in the study of previously undescribed languages (or, sometimes, in the re-description of previously described languages that they feel to be in need of description from a new perspective). Dirty-feet linguists are, of course, not frequently referred to as such, though speaking as an enthusiastic career-long field linguist myself, I can confirm that it usually takes several days of soaking and scrubbing to remove the ingrained dirt from the soles of my feet after a few months spent shoeless in the field. Field linguists typically fall into the 'broad-surface' approach to the study of linguistic universals in that we stress the need for reliable descriptive observations from as broad a range of languages as possible in order to make deductions about what is and what is not possible in human language.

Dirty-feet linguists provide the fodder upon which many armchair linguists depend. While there is a long tradition of linguistic fieldwork in North America that dates back to the period of Sapir and Bloomfield in the 1920s and 1930s, American universities since the Chomskyan revolution of the 1960s have for the most part been dominated by armchair formalists. European universities are similarly dominated by the armchair tradition. In many of these universities, fieldwork-based dissertations in linguistics are sometimes discouraged as being 'too descriptive', or as being insufficiently informed by theory.

In Australia, however, the fieldwork tradition is alive and well, reflecting the enduring influence of R. M. W. Dixon who was influential in establishing the modern grammar-writing tradition in that country after his first academic appointment there in 1970. In Australian universities, the tradition has developed of a linguist going out to the field and 'doing' a language for his or her doctoral dissertation. That was certainly how I gained my doctorate: I 'did' Bandjalang as part of my undergraduate training (Crowley 1978), and then I 'did' the Paamese language of Vanuatu for my Ph.D. (Crowley 1982). Fortunately, there are plenty of universities elsewhere in the world reflecting the same grammar-writing tradition, despite the seemingly irresistible power of the armchair formalists in some places.

Armchair linguists and dirty-feet linguists tend to look down on followers of the other tradition. Dirty-feet linguists typically characterize armchair formalists as being out of touch with reality, as dealing with introspective and intuitive data that has not been subject to empirical verification, and as delving often into theoretical trivia. Armchair linguists tend to look down on their dirty-feet counterparts because they feel that they fail to carry out analysis at sufficient levels of derivational depth, and because they often do not include in their descriptions any discussions of constructions which reflect any level of theoretical sophistication.

In reality, of course, this kind of enmity is unnecessary and unhelpful (Foley 1993, Gil 2001: 125–8). No descriptive fieldworker can carry out linguistic analysis of a previously undescribed language in a theoretical vacuum. We therefore need the insights that theoretical linguistics can offer in order to guide our search for new data, and to influence our analysis of that data. Similarly, no theoretician can offer valid generalizations without access to a wide range of reliable descriptive data. So, new linguistic descriptions will always need to be written, and theoretical discussions will forever need to be re-evaluated in the light of these descriptions.

1.2.2 Fieldwork at home and fieldwork in The Field

There is a kind of halfway house in linguistic fieldwork between sitting in the armchair and getting dirty feet. Those of you who have done a university Field Methods course have already been there. I have seen some academic curricula vitae in which linguists have stated that they have 'done fieldwork' on such-and-such a language, though in reality they may have travelled no further than the outer suburbs of San Francisco or Manchester.

While this is clearly a *kind* of fieldwork, it is not really the kind of fieldwork that I will be primarily dealing with in this volume. At most, this kind of fieldwork is useful if you are only interested in studying a particular feature of a language without intending to produce a coherent overall account. If, on the other hand, you are planning on producing a comprehensive account of a language, this kind of fieldwork might represent a legitimate initial foray to prepare yourself for the real task of going out into the community where the language is spoken. As part of any preparation for a field trip, you should certainly try to find a speaker of the language in your own area before you leave. Particularly in a university community, there are likely to be people from many parts of the world, and there may turn out to be a member of the language community that you have chosen living nearby. Such a person can also help you to become familiar with the general situation in the language area. And of course, such a person may even be able to help you to get started in the field by introducing you to people within his or her home community. Being introduced by an insider can, after all, be a huge benefit.

But should you consider doing *all* of your fieldwork without leaving home? Any work that you do with a speaker of a language other than English with a view to publishing the resulting linguistic analysis can legitimately be referred to as fieldwork. Fieldwork 'at home' like this has many advantages for the field linguist. I have found that regular short sessions with a speaker of a language where you can work at home with an ergonomic chair and desk, electric lights, and a computer nearby on which you can regularly update your analysis as new material comes in can be an extremely productive way to work on a language.

However, there are real drawbacks associated with this approach. If you were to write a linguistic description on the basis of information from just a single speaker and you do not have the advantage of being able to observe natural interactions between speakers, you run the risk of missing some elements of the language. One problem is that the context of elicitation may not be sufficiently varied pragmatically to produce a full range of constructions or vocabulary. There is also a real danger that your single speaker may end up effectively 'filtering' out certain kinds of constructions because he or she is subconsciously evaluating how good a command of the language you have acquired, and judging what kinds of structures you are ready to deal with. This means that it is essential in a good linguistic description for data to come not just from direct elicit-ation or from what is recorded in narrative texts, but it must come also from observations of casual utterances between people speaking spon-taneously around you.

Let me show you what I mean with an actual example. In a description of one language that was described on the basis of information from a single speaker 'at home', instrumental noun phrases (INST) are described as being marked by means of a particular preposition according to the pattern:

I washed my clothes INST *soap.*

With third person singular inanimate noun phrases, the pronoun is usually expressed as zero. Thus, in order to say 'I washed my clothes with it', you would say the equivalent of something like:

I washed my clothes INST.

So far, so good, in that there is nothing that is inaccurate in what the final grammar ended up saying.

After the grammar was completed, the dissertation was examined, and it was deposited for posterity in the library, conversational data gathered within the community where the language was regularly spoken revealed that when the object of the preposition is fronted to the beginning of the clause—as happens often in spontaneous speech for a variety of reasons—then the instrumental preposition is very often shifted so that it appears between the verb and its object, resulting in patterns such as the following:

This is the soap that I washed INST *my clothes.*

This construction would probably never appear in sentences translated directly from English, as the more English-like construction below still represents a grammatically acceptable possibility:

This is the soap that I wash my clothes INST.

In this case, the narrative texts which formed the basis of much of the grammar did not provide enough variation in the pragmatic contexts for these kinds of constructions to appear. The grammar, therefore, ended up being incomplete.

So, fieldwork should ideally be conducted within the community where the language is used in order to ensure access to a sufficiently rich and varied set of data. A more pure-minded fieldworker might also want to argue in any case that fieldwork at home in the comfort of your living room involves insufficient levels of self-deprivation. There is a part of me which says that for your grammar to be truly worthy, you must have suffered at least one bout of malaria—or some other impressive-sounding tropical ailment—in its writing, or you should have had at least one toenail ripped off by your hiking boots, or you should have developed a nasty boil on an unmentionable part of your body. I, of course, have suffered all of these misfortunes in the field, and many more. And, by golly, if I had to go through this, then I feel that everybody else should have to suffer to a similar extent!

Further reading: Hyman (2001).

1.3 What kind of linguistics?

Some descriptive linguists define basic linguistic documentation as reflecting the very essence of the discipline of linguistics, which they regard as taking precedence over all other areas of linguistic activity:

The ideal apprenticeship [for a linguist] is to undertake fieldwork on some previously undescribed (or scarcely described) language—recording, transcribing and analysing texts; observing how people use the language in the daily round; writing a grammar and phonology; compiling a dictionary; and publishing a volume of annotated texts. (Dixon 2001)

There are probably as many different ways of describing the phonology, morphology, and syntax of a language as there are linguists, though different approaches can often be gathered roughly under a variety of different theoretical labels. Linguistic descriptions that are rigidly bound to particular theoretical constructs do not tend successfully to outlast the theories which spawned them. Grammars that are written, for example, according to the strict structuralist formulae that were in vogue up to the early 1960s, or according to the transformational model which became all the rage immediately after this, are often extremely difficult for people to read today. Similarly, descriptions that are expressed exclusively in terms that derive from some of today's theoretical traditions are often equally unreadable to those who hail from other traditions.

The most readable—and arguably, therefore, the most valuable—accounts of languages seem to be those which are relatively open to theoretical eclecticism. By this, I mean that a linguistic description should set out to allow the linguistic data to govern the form of the description, rather than requiring a single theoretical model rigidly to dictate the shape of the entire grammar. Some would argue that there is a single theory-neutral model for grammatical description which can be used for any language, as implied by Dixon's (1997: 128–38) use of the expression Basic Linguistic Theory. While it would perhaps be nice if this were the case, any linguistic description is in reality going to exhibit certain kinds of theoretical biases, many of which may be implicit. The most important consideration in producing a good linguistic description is that the writer's particular theoretical assumptions should be clearly recognizable to the reader, that any terminological conventions should be clearly explained, and that the grammar should be richly exemplified with natural data so that readers coming from other theoretical persuasions are able to make sense of your discussion. With new technological tools it is possible to create rich contextual data in a media corpus for which your analysis provides a gateway (e.g. Thieberger 2004) and which allows others to confirm and extend your analysis.

Linguistics is a hugely diverse discipline, and field linguists can contribute to our knowledge in a wide variety of ways. While most linguists are primarily interested in matters of phonology, morphology, and syntax, the ways in which language is used 'in the daily round' noted by Dixon seldom receive more than passing mention. Only a minority of linguists—better, perhaps, linguistic anthropologists—have shown themselves to be interested in documenting how language functions as a 'mode of social interaction [which] provides the material out of which a group of people recognize themselves as a community' (Duranti 1997: 99). Such accounts cannot be based on the traditional direct 'elicitation' of language data from 'informants'; rather, the fieldworker must become a long-term participant observer, recording extensive collections of both audio and video data of natural language use between different individuals within the community.

At the same time, it is clear that Duranti's (1994) discussion of the ways in which grammatical constructions in Samoan are used to achieve socio-political goals depends crucially on a prior analysis of the language in a traditional descriptive account such as that of Mosel and Hovdhaugen (1992). Even the title of Duranti's linguistic anthropological account—*From Grammar to Politics*—implies this priority. Similarly, Schieffelin and Ochs (1986) show how language acquisition by children is related to socialization into different cultures using the same kinds of basic linguistic information. Traditional descriptive accounts, then, should be promoted as an essential stepping stone for bigger—and some would no doubt argue, better—things.

The goals of fieldwork can sometimes be much more limited than a full published grammar or dictionary, or a detailed ethnographic account of the communicative strategies that are used by people in a particular society. Sometimes, previously published materials may spark the interest of specialists who return to somebody else's previous field site in order to analyse some particular features of the language in more detail. For instance, in some of the languages of Vanuatu, there are phonemically contrastive linguo-labial consonants in which nasals, stops, and fricatives are produced with the tip of the tongue touching the upper lips. Ian Maddieson undertook a fieldtrip from the United States to Vanuatu in the 1980s simply to study these speech sounds in detail in a number of languages in which they are found. A guide that is specifically geared towards instrumental phonetics is beyond the scope of this volume, though Ladefoged (2003) and Maddieson (2001) provide a great deal of very readable material.

Published grammars concentrate for the most part on regular patterns, resulting in a lack of attention devoted to the study of patterns of variable data. There is absolutely no reason why the kinds of corpus-based statistical studies that have been carried out extensively on different varieties of English could not be carried out in other languages as well, e.g. Dorian's (2001) work on Gaelic. However, in order to do this, a linguist would need to pay close attention to a much wider range of sampling and data-gathering issues than is commonly done in order to ensure that statistically representative samples of different categories of speakers have been recorded. While I have also decided to exclude sociolinguistic studies from the scope of this volume, readers who are interested in an up-to-date guide to data-gathering of this kind could consult Milroy (1987).

1.4 Anthropological and linguistic fieldwork

The threat to the world's linguistic diversity to which I have already referred is not a threat that we have only recently become aware of.

In North America in the late nineteenth century, people realized that things were not well. People saw that traditional knowledge, belief systems, and languages were about to be irretrievably lost with the passing of the last generations of Native Americans who were born before the push by European Americans to occupy the West.

Part of the response to this realization was the establishment of the Boasian tradition of anthropological fieldwork which involved for the first time academics from North American universities going out to stay in different communities in order to find out how people lived, what they believed, and how they spoke. Franz Boas (1911: 60) himself regarded a command of the language as 'an indispensable means of obtaining accurate and thorough [ethnographic] knowledge'. Edward Sapir was drawn into this fieldwork tradition, and while he was in part a traditional anthropologist, he was also a gifted linguist. He contributed a number of substantial original descriptions of previously undescribed languages, while at the same time playing an important role in developing a methodology for describing new languages.

While anthropology and linguistics began very much as kindred disciplines at the time of Boas and Sapir, they have diverged quite substantially in the meantime to the point where these days, the stereotypical ethnographer and the stereotypical linguist aim to produce quite different outputs and they often go about their fieldwork in quite different sorts of ways. Anthropologists often aim for a much more modest speaking ability in the language, in spite of Malinowski's (1929: 465) warning that:

There has been no greater source of error in Anthropology than the use of misunderstood and misinterpreted fragments of native vocabulary by observers not thoroughly conversant with native tongues and ignorant of the sociological nature of language.

Margaret Mead wrote of the importance of a knowledge of the local language in carrying out anthropological fieldwork, yet she apparently had a far from sophisticated command of Samoan despite the fact that much of her anthropological reputation derived from her work in American Samoa. Her work has in recent years been subject to intense debate, with her command of the language being subject to scrutiny (Freeman 1983: 286, Holmes 1987: 112). Michael Goldsmsith (pers. comm.) reports that at a public lecture that Margaret Mead once gave in Fiji, a Samoan woman stood up and pointed out that many Samoans did not agree with some of the things that she had written about them. Rather than engaging in debate about the serious issues being raised, Mead's response was to offer the formulaic *Fa'afetai, fa'afetai lava, fa'afetai tele lava* 'Thank you very very much', which evidently impressed the non-Samoans in the audience, but it hardly represented a staggering display of linguistic virtuosity.

Despite these differences between linguistics and anthropology, there is a very real sense in which no field linguist can fail to be part-anthropologist, and no field anthropologist can fail to be part-linguist. Any linguist who aims to learn to acquire a speaking knowledge of the language that he or she is studying clearly has to understand at least some of the cultural norms of the community in order to understand what people mean by what they are saying. Any anthropologist who cannot, to some extent at least, overhear what people are saying in their ordinary conversations with each other is entirely dependent on his or her own direct questions for an understanding of local cultural practices.

Arguably, the field linguist has something of an advantage over the field ethnographer in terms of our final outputs, as we linguists know pretty well what sorts of things we should set out to discover as soon as we get to our field sites. We know, for example, that whatever language we are going to study, it must have phonemes. We won't know how many phonemes there will be, or what shape they might have, but we can be absolutely certain that there will be phonemes. We also know that those phonemes will go together to make up morphemes, which will in turn make up words, and these will in turn be put together to make up phrases and sentences. We can be certain about all of this because every language in the world, by definition, has a hierarchically organized grammar.

Obviously, the kinds of meanings that are going to be distinguished by the morphemes of any given language are something that we will have to work out from scratch when we get into the field, as well as the way in which the grammar is organized, but we know exactly where to start. We linguists therefore arrive in the field with a rough series of chapter and section headings already set in our minds: Consonants, Vowels, Phonotactics, Morphophonemics, Noun Phrases, Pronouns, Possession, Relative Clauses, Verbs, Adverbs, Simple Sentences, Complex Sentences, and so on. Obviously, we have to do some fine-tuning, perhaps abandoning some of the headings that we arrived with and introducing new headings in order to accommodate particular features of the language that we are dealing with. But the fact remains that we have some kind of broad framework upon which we can hang the various facts that we are about to discover. There are even published guides to tell us what sorts of possibilities we can expect to encounter along the way (Shopen 1985*a*, 1985*b*, 1985*c*, Payne 1997, Whaley 1997).

By way of contrast, the task of the anthropologist is much more open-ended. While there are reportedly somewhere between 11 and 141 phonemes in all of the known languages of the world, there is nothing that is remotely parallel to this unit of analysis in the study of culture. If there were, then all behaviour within any given cultural group could ultimately be broken down into a combination of a highly restricted number of individual 'behaviouremes', which could then be combined in set ways into larger behavioural units. Anthropologists have in the past exhibited some envy for linguists and their phonemes and they have invoked the linguistic distinction between etics and emics in their own work. However, an ethnographer cannot arrive in the field with anything similar to the chapter and section headings of linguists.

2

Ethical Issues

When I went on my first linguistic fieldtrip in the early 1970s, there was no expectation that I would have to prepare a submission for the ethical approval for project. How times have changed! It is now *de rigueur* for any research proposal that involves human subjects to pass scrutiny from the appropriate Ethics Committee. Most linguistic research that is aimed at documenting little-known languages, if it is conducted at all sensitively and sensibly, should not face any serious challenges from an Ethics Committee. However, there are some important ethical issues to which any researcher should give serious thought, including a number of issues that go beyond what any Ethics Committee will ordinarily be expected to deal with.

2.1 Linguists and speakers

First and foremost among the ethical obligations of a field linguist are those which involve his or her relationship with the people from whom the linguistic data will be recorded. It is this relationship which an Ethics Committee will normally be primarily involved with.

2.1.1 Ethical guidelines

Any responsible research institution these days is certain to have its own specific guidelines for the submission of applications for the ethical approval of research which involves human subjects, as well as a system for overseeing these guidelines, including an Ethics Committee which is charged with overseeing individual research projects involving human subjects. Moreover, any outside funding agency is likely to make any granting of funds for projects dealing with human subjects conditional upon the ethical approval of the project by an appropriate committee.

Different national Linguistic Societies have often established sets of ethical guidelines for the conduct of linguistic research within their own countries, or by that society's members while carrying out research in other countries. You should consult with your own country's Linguistic Society—as well as the Linguistic Society in the country in which you plan to conduct your research—to see if they can provide you with documents setting out issues that you should aim to address in your project. These points will typically be geared specifically towards Linguistics as a discipline.

If you are planning on carrying out research in a country other than the one in which you are based, you may also need to gain ethical approval from a relevant body in that country. If you have never been to the country before, it may be difficult for you to find out what the procedures are, but a relevant diplomatic mission or a creative search on the internet should hopefully lead to the kinds of documents that you need.

Generally, the guidelines of such a committee will seek to ensure that:

- information which is provided by an individual is not made public in a way that is harmful either to himself/herself or to others;
- anybody from whom you will be gathering linguistic data should be properly informed of the nature of your research project;
- anybody who you approach should be free to agree to participate in the project without any pressure from the researcher, and that he or she should be free to withdraw from participation at any time without having to offer any explanation for this decision.

These kinds of issues should in most cases be easy enough to address if you are aiming to produce a straightforward grammatical description of a language, along with a dictionary or an accompanying collection of texts. However, there are some possible pitfalls, which I will address in turn.

If you are unlucky enough to receive an initial response from your Ethics Committee that seems to you to show a particular lack of linguistic awareness, just remember that this may not necessarily be all the fault of the committee members. It may be, in fact, that your original submission lacked some essential background information which you incorrectly assumed that non-linguists would already know. You should respond by carefully providing the requested additional information and resubmit your proposal.

2.1.2 Avoiding harm

You will need to demonstrate to your Ethics Committee that you are aware of any possible circumstances in which your research may result in harm either to those who have provided you with information, or to others. It is almost unimaginable that harm could arise to anybody as a result of the recording of everyday words for ordinary things. Similarly, many of the stories that you record as part of your research will be intended primarily for enjoyment, amusement, or to provide moral lessons for children. These kinds of stories are also unlikely to result in harm to anybody. You should be aware, however, that what may appear to be an innocent children's tale recorded for posterity could later be construed by that community as, for example, a claim for land based on the speaker's knowledge of the story and that story's association with spirits inhabiting certain areas of land.

Because linguistics at many universities is a relatively small discipline, there may well not be a representative from this discipline on your own Ethics Committee. You may find that you are facing the task of trying to get your project approved by a committee that is more used to vetting proposals from Psychology or Sociology, where people may be soliciting attitudes about highly sensitive issues such as transsexuality, spouse abuse, internet pornography, or addiction to illegal drugs. The public release of personal information obtained in interviews in such circumstances clearly *does* have the potential to harm either the interviewee or other people. Because our discipline is very often poorly understood by academics from other disciplines, it may occasionally turn out to be surprisingly difficult to convince committee members that the person who is going to tell you that the word for 'dog' in the Eastern Rainforest language is *siliwan* is not subjecting himself or herself to unspeakable potential harm in providing you with this information.

However, you do need to understand that some of the things that linguists do in the field *can* be damaging. Your description of the language could, in principle, be based on nothing but recordings of slanderous lies about other people. After all, we use the same grammar and vocabulary when we are lying that we use when we are telling the truth and these kinds of utterances would represent linguistically valid data. Such recordings would, of course, be quite damaging if anybody else ever heard them, so you will need to ensure that you avoid recording any information of this kind that is known to be untruthful and hurtful.

Avoiding harm in the stories that you record goes beyond the need to avoid deliberate untruths. I remember being told one story while carrying out fieldwork in Vanuatu that was highly entertaining and, I thought, well worth adding to my collection of stories. As soon as I suggested that we proceed to record the story on tape, the narrator baulked. The story was about some people who always did things the opposite way to ordinary people. So, instead of eating the flesh of yams, they just ate the skin, instead of using pigs as exchange at weddings, they married them, and so on. My presumption was that these were mythical beings of some kind, but it turns out that in local tradition, these were seen as the ancestors of a particular lineage on the island, and this lineage included the local member of parliament at the time. Although everybody on the island knew these stories, it was felt that to document them in writing risked insulting this important person, and this might have opened up all manner of political divisions that were lurking just below the surface. A visiting linguist should clearly not be seen as provoking this kind of controversy, so I did not pursue the issue of recording these stories on tape.

Oral tradition in traditional non-literate societies often also serves the purpose of providing a link between people and places by establishing ancestry. While it might appear to the outsider-linguist that a story about a family that is descended from some particular animal might be little more than a story, it may well be that this story is implicitly taken by local people to indicate that the family involved has rights to land in whatever places are associated with the pig in the story. Such stories may be entirely uncontroversial locally if there happen to be no disputes or disagreements over the land in question. However, you may well be unaware that members of another family assert *their* link to the same land via a different story, or perhaps even by the same story, but with a few particular twists.

I recently quite innocently recorded, transcribed, edited, and distributed a story for which I was given no indication that it might relate in any way to a local land dispute. When I returned to my field site on my next visit, I was taken aside by a member of the family on the opposite side of the dispute who explained that his family felt that their position on a local land dispute had been misrepresented in the story. Fortunately, the version that I had sent out was only a draft that was not very widely distributed. I was able to apologize and I promised to excise the story from any collections of stories that I might distribute more widely in future. Things could easily have been much worse, and publicizing a story unwisely could result in the welcome mat being removed by the community. I don't personally know of any linguists who have been 'dis-invited' from the community in which they were based, but I have heard of anthropologists to whom this has happened.

2.1.3 Informed consent

Before your work gets under way, you will need to provide useful information about your project to people from whom you are going to be gathering data. In some societies, this may turn out to be quite difficult. Even explaining what you mean by a grammatical description of their language, if that is what you are aiming to produce, will often be far from easy. People will almost certainly not know what you mean by 'phonology', 'morphology', and 'syntax', so any attempt to solicit informed consent should avoid such notions. And if your primary interests are, for example, in matters such as split ergativity and its relationship with animacy in noun phrases, then explaining this in any kind of meaningful way to a linguistically naive audience is almost certainly a lost cause from the outset. It is best, therefore, not even to try.

What you will need to do instead is describe your intentions in terms that people *are* likely readily to understand, while at the same time not being misleading. It has been necessary in my experience sometimes to say to people something like 'I have come to write your language'. Given that your project will almost certainly entail gathering lexical data, and gathering narrative texts in written form as a basis for grammatical analysis, you can satisfy your participants' need to be properly informed by describing your project in these terms.

Since you will also be attempting to 'learn the language by collecting words and stories', you can also tell people that this is what your plans involve. Sometimes people have asked if I have come 'to translate the language', to which I can truthfully answer that I have—though it has sometimes been necessary to add that I would not be 'translating the Bible' into the language, as people have sometimes assumed (and hoped). I am certainly not the only linguist who has been faced with assumptions about religious motivations. Lyle Campbell (pers. comm.) reports that in Central America, sometimes the only reason that people would agree to

share their linguistic knowledge with him was their belief that he was
a priest, even though he had previously told them he was not.

2.1.4 Voluntary participation

When human subjects are being interviewed within your own community
for research projects in history, sociology, geography, and suchlike, your
Ethics Committee is very likely to insist that participants be provided
with a written consent form that each participant is expected to sign.
While this may be unproblematic with many non-linguistic projects, there
can sometimes be real problems with this when conducting linguistic
field research.

For one thing, one excellent way of recording linguistic information is
to note things as they are said in natural spoken contexts rather than in
a formal interview situation. It is quite impractical to insist that
somebody who has just spontaneously used a particularly interesting—
and previously unknown—word or grammatical construction in your
presence be asked to stop speaking so that you can have them sign a
consent form in retrospect before they be allowed to continue speaking so
that you can write down what you have just heard. After all, you are not
interested in the content of what has been said; rather, you are merely
interested in the manner in which that content was expressed.

While it might be appropriate to ask people in highly literate urban
societies to sign informed consent forms when they are participating in
interview-like direct elicitation, there are potential problems associated
with this in the less literate and predominantly rural societies in which
much linguistic fieldwork is carried out. One of the overriding principles
of ethical research is that the researcher should avoid any potential harm
to the subject. However, in a society in which an inability to read and write
may be reasonably common, it may cause considerable embarrassment
when someone is asked to sign a form that he or she cannot read, or when
that person may not even be able to sign their name.

The problems do not end there. Even if an individual can read and
write, it is possible that in a society where literacy is relatively marginal
and where quite different sets of social assumptions are associated with an
ability to read and write, asking people to sign a formal document may
raise more doubts and suspicions about a project than a simple verbal
approval to participate. In some of the rural societies where I have been

working in Vanuatu, for example, the only legal documents that most people have ever had to sign are contracts with overseas logging companies. These contracts are then not infrequently broken unilaterally by the companies involved, leading to all manner of nastiness. Associating linguistic research in the minds of participants with these kinds of disputes is arguably a very bad idea.

In the absence of signed consent forms, some Ethics Committees may be happy for formal approval to be given by an appropriate person or institution on behalf of participating individuals. This may involve a chief, or perhaps a council of chiefs, or some other local equivalent, where the chiefs traditionally operate only with the consent of community members rather than operating dictatorially. On the other hand, if you feel that you can ask for a signed consent form, then you could include a paragraph outlining the speaker's expectations about how the records you make will be used. For example, you could include a statement that the recordings will be used for educational and not for commercial purposes. As you will no doubt be depositing your tapes in a linguistic archive it is a good idea to clarify who can listen to them so that the archive can keep the data according to your and your speakers' wishes.

Ethics Committees may also ask the researcher to get people to signal their willingness to participate verbally in a recording. Even without being asked to do this, I have found that when people offer to record a story for transcription, their stories often begin with words to the following effect, which clearly signal their willing participation:

My name is so-and-so and I want to tell a story about such-and-such.

Even where the speaker does not specifically mention his or her own name, I always record an introductory opening message which says something like the following in a language that the participant can understand:

Today's date is such-and-such and I am in such-and-such a place, with so-and-so who is going to tell a story in his/her language.

As long as the narrator clearly signals agreement with my introduction with words such as the following, this can certainly be construed as an expression of consent which should satisfy the needs of an Ethics Committee:

I want to tell a story about such-and-such.

2.1.5 Money and fieldwork

To produce a substantial description of any language is likely to take several years of your time, but it is also going to involve quite a commitment of time from your language-helpers in the field. In traditional rural societies, life can often be a struggle. People may have to hunt and fish for their meat, they may have to watch over their cattle, they may have to plant and tend their crops, and they may have to gather firewood and fetch water. This can all be extremely hard work, and in such societies nobody can afford the luxury of indolence. I learned this the hard way on my last fieldtrip to Malakula when the mother of the family that I was staying with went to visit her sons in town for a few months. Suddenly I found myself occasionally having to take charge of preparing food and cooking over an open fire for working parties of fifteen hungry men who were building a house for the family. I certainly got no language work done on those days.

Any demands that you make on somebody's time to help you with your project almost certainly eat into time that he or she would have devoted to other more life-sustaining activities. You will therefore need to be somewhat flexible about the time that you plan to work together to allow your language-helper to see to his or her own needs from time to time. There is also a question of compensation for that person's time.

The budget for your project must include provision for the payment of language-helpers at a locally appropriate rate. Sometimes, local rates of pay may seem unrealistically low to somebody who has spent their entire life in a major western city. However, to insist on offering rates of pay similar to what you would pay for fieldwork help in New York when you are in a tiny rural village somewhere in Cameroon is certainly not going to fix any of the fundamental economic inequities that have brought this about. Moreover, paying people more than the going rate is likely to cause problems for future workers. Dimmendaal (2001: 59) reports that in one situation in Ethiopia, a foreign film crew with a large budget paid local people at high rates, which local people expected to be matched by linguists who arrived later, even though they were operating with a much more limited budget.

While paying a wage may often be entirely appropriate and very much appreciated, you may need to become sensitive to local ways of giving money to people. In Vanuatu, for example, you never hand cash over to somebody in public, even if it is their money that you are repaying from a loan. Cash is normally discreetly proffered inside your hand with only the back of your hand visible. Alternatively, you can hand over cash to somebody inside an envelope.

Direct payment of cash can of course sometimes cause embarrassment. I had been working sporadically with one man on the transcription and translation of texts. Christmas was approaching and I knew that people in the village were finding things tough that year because copra prices had fallen. I therefore discreetly offered him a cash payment. He initially refused, saying that he was happy to help me with my project because of its importance in the community. I ended up having to reassure him that the payment was only fair, and in any case, it was not my own money, but it was money that had been set aside as part of the project. To signal the official—rather than personal—nature of the transaction, I asked him to sign my receipt book for me.

While some people may be embarrassed about accepting cash, you can expect to encounter others who may be rather more mercenary. I remember one man who was well known in the community I was working in for latching onto relatives from town who had jobs. Inevitably there would be a request for money. A visiting linguist, of course, is also fair game, especially if it is known that he or she has given cash to somebody else who has been working on the linguistic project. I could see this man constantly watching me so he could catch me alone. Once, when he had successfully cornered me, he started talking about fingers, and the names in the local language for each of the five fingers. I had already recorded these words, and although I could guess where this was leading, I could see no easy way out. Eventually, he asked me straight up if I would pay him for these finger-words. Fortunately, our privacy was disturbed when somebody else happened along at just the right time and local mores dictated that talk of money had to cease. If that had not happened, I might have had little choice but to get myself out of this awkward situation by buying this man a packet of cigarettes.

Sometimes, it may be necessary to be flexible about the manner of compensation for somebody's time, as direct cash payments may not always be appropriate. It is best to be sensitive to local practices and if payment in kind seems more appropriate, then you can by all means offer people some kind of gift instead. I had been working with one rather old lady on Erromango. While her mind was razor sharp, she was sufficiently frail that even a trip to the local store to spend cash would have been quite taxing. It was suggested that it would be more appropriate for me to buy her a length of cloth, a few packets of sugar, and some blocks of laundry soap rather than offer her straight cash, and that is what I did. (Local tradition dictated that a gift such as mine be reciprocated. This lady picked up her walking stick and hobbled over to her basket where she kept her money. She took out a note and handed it to me. While I felt uncomfortable about accepting this, I was relieved to note that her return gift was substantially less than the cash value of my original offering.)

You also need to appreciate that in many rural areas, even with cash in hand there is often a limit to what is available in local stores. People may therefore prefer gifts that you have brought in from town where the stores are better stocked. I have also found that a gift that is bought overseas rather than in one of the local stores sometimes has a mystique about it that makes it so much more appreciated. I have tried arguing that a Seiko watch that is bought in New Zealand is the same Seiko watch that can be bought in the local capital (where it is sometimes even cheaper), but people still persist in placing orders for me to buy things in New Zealand.

I therefore often accede to hints—or direct requests—for all manner of items, as long as the cost is not excessive, and transport is not an issue. This has included items as varied as liquor, clothes, shoes, watches, cassette-radios, and even a tent and a pair of binoculars. Of course, this kind of payment can make for some difficulties in accounting. Your home institution may require proper receipts for every penny that you have spent, yet you can hardly give somebody a gift and then ask them to sign a receipt for it. You may therefore need to acquire some skills in creative accounting by shifting the cost of such gifts under some other heading.

Further reading: Dimmendaal (2001), Samarin (1967: 20–44), Bouquiaux and Thomas (1992:36), Vaux and Cooper (1999:13).

2.1.6 Ethical delinquency

While linguistic research in the field should ordinarily not present too many ethical problems in terms of your relationship to the individuals who are providing your data, some linguistic projects in the past have been problematic, and this has caused difficulties for others down the line. For instance, there was once a serious proposal in Papua New Guinea to gather together a number of monolingual people from structurally diverse languages in what came to be referred to as the Desert Island Experiment. The intention was to provide these people each with the same small vocabulary and see how their communicative needs within this artificially created community came to be handled over a twelve-month period. The ultimate aim was to study the process of pidginization with a view to finding out what sorts of grammatical structures emerged.

There were, however, some very serious ethical problems with this project as it was formulated. The monolingual Papua New Guineans who were needed for the project to succeed would necessarily have been uneducated, as well as coming from very remote communities. They would therefore have had little contact with the outside world, and would almost certainly have had little idea about how scientists conduct their experiments. Explaining the nature of the project and gaining people's voluntary informed consent would therefore have been extremely difficult given that these people would not have been speakers of any lingua franca. In the end, this project was canned—quite rightly so—after having been condemned by linguists and political authorities in Papua New Guinea for its exploitative and inherently unethical nature.

Few linguistic research projects of which I am aware have exhibited anything like this level of human exploitation, and linguists have for the most part tended to be seen as fairly harmless sorts of drudges who collect obscure words and grammatical constructions. However, we do sometimes get confused with anthropologists, and sometimes anthropologists are confused with commercial artefact collectors or film-makers. In some places people have felt betrayed by the actions of such commercial activities, and this may be reflected in a reluctance to participate in linguistic research. It may therefore be necessary to explain in some detail precisely what sorts of things you are interested in, and what you are *not* intending to do.

2.2 Linguists and communities

In addition to any general ethical responsibilities towards the individual human subjects who participate in your research that may be governed by the formal requirements of your Ethics Committee, any linguist also needs to accept that they have a number of broader ethical obligations vis-à-vis the language community as a whole.

Some countries—or parts of countries—have in the past declared themselves closed to foreign researchers for several years because researchers in the past had failed to produce copies of materials that they have produced for members of the community to see and use. This has included some linguists who have been seen collecting vocabulary and oral traditions for some years, without publishing their results, or even distributing informally produced copies for the benefit of members of the language community. To people in the community, it looked very much as if the linguist was taking material away, and not giving anything back to the community in return. Vanuatu was one country which declared a research moratorium over an extended period for these sorts of reasons.

Research opportunities have opened up again in Vanuatu, but the approval of linguistic research is now subject to a requirement that the researcher sign a legally binding contract with the Vanuatu Cultural Centre, which states (among other things) that:

All research projects will include a cultural product of *immediate benefit and use* to the local community.... Such projects could include booklets of kastom [i.e. traditional] information, photo albums of visual records, simple educational booklets for use in schools... programs for the revitalisation of particular kastom skills in the community, training workshops in cultural documentation, etc.

We researchers should therefore consider ourselves obligated to provide something for the community in which we have done our work. What we provide for the community by way of feedback should be something that will be valued by members of the community, as well as being of some kind of practical benefit to people in the community.

2.2.1 Grammars

A researcher needs to be aware that in many situations a grammatical description by itself will not satisfy the kinds of expectations that members of a community may have. This is because most grammars are by and large not comprehensible to non-specialists, and some grammars are comprehensible only to small coteries of linguists who adopt very specific theoretical assumptions and terminology. Given that most linguists are primarily interested in grammatical research, while most communities are more likely to be interested in other kinds of linguistic research outputs, there is a real potential for conflict between community and academy in descriptive linguistic research projects. This is still something of an unresolved issue, and it is one that any intending researcher needs to be well aware of in order to take the appropriate steps to keep the conflict of interests to a minimum.

Let me illustrate this point with a personal example. Between 1994 and 1998, I was conducting research on the island of Erromango in Vanuatu. My primary academic interests were as follows, ranked in the order given:

- the production of a grammar of the actively spoken Sye language;
- the production of a grammar of the moribund Ura language;
- the production of a bilingual Sye–English dictionary;
- the production of a bilingual Ura–English dictionary.

These interests—and their ranking—are governed in part by the academic law of publish-or-perish. This dictum is increasingly being formalized in universities as some kind of 'research quantum' that is subject to external audit, with government funding being dependent on scores across the university. That is, I—and nowadays also my university—stand to gain more academic brownie points by analysing the grammatical system of a language than I would by publishing an alphabetized list of words and their meanings.

There was also an issue of personal preference here, as I am more interested in describing a viable language than a moribund one. I could immerse myself into a social context in which Sye was spoken naturally around me. I could form friendships where Sye was a daily medium of exchange and I could learn about a new culture through its language. With moribund Ura, however, I could not expect to have the same kinds of interactions. First, the handful of speakers of Ura were dispersed across several villages rather than being concentrated in a single community. Second, most speakers of Ura were quite old and no longer very mobile. This meant that there was not much prospect of 'hanging out' with speakers and this did not seem very appealing to me.

However, judging by what people said to me on Erromango, community expectations from my research seemed to be as follows (in the order given):

- the production of a written collection of oral traditions in Sye;
- the production of an Ura–Sye or an Ura–Bislama dictionary;
- the production of a Sye dictionary of some kind.

You will see that a grammar of neither Sye nor Ura figured at all in community expectations. While the word 'dictionary' is widely known on Erromango, the word 'grammar' is probably only known to a very small number of people who have tertiary or upper secondary education. In fact, even those educated people who know the word 'grammar' may think that it is something that applies only to English. I remember eliciting a series of verbal paradigms from a speaker of Gela, a language of the Solomon Islands. Eventually, when it dawned on him what I was doing, his eyes lit up and he said, 'Oh, I never knew that my language had a grammar.'

People on Erromango are aware that much oral tradition has been retained by the older generation, and that the earlier practice of passing down stories at night around the fire is disappearing. To ensure that generations to come have access to these stories, people wanted to see these stories recorded on tape, as well as in writing. The Vanuatu Cultural Centre has for many years provided training and recording equipment to enable local people to do this kind of recording. However, in the tropical climate of this island, which has no proper tape storage facilities—nor even any electricity—such material quickly deteriorates. Material has been deposited in safe storage facilities in the Vanuatu Cultural Centre archive in the capital, but for years the lack of cataloguing has meant that once material is deposited, it can easily become inaccessible to all but the most determined. In any case, the archives are located on another island, which is an expensive forty-five-minute flight away from Erromango. Thus, recording material on tape by itself does not ensure the survival of oral traditions; rather, it simply 'museumizes' them. Providing an accessible written record of oral tradition therefore obviates these problems.

Erromangans' interest in an Ura–Sye or Ura–Bislama dictionary is also perfectly understandable. In the last century, Ura was widely spoken in the northern part of the island. However, massive depopulation and resulting demographic realignments in the nineteenth and early twentieth centuries have resulted in a situation where there are today only about half a dozen elderly speakers of Ura left. It is clear to everybody that this is a highly endangered language. The major language of the island today is Sye. All adults on the island are also able to speak Bislama, the national language of Vanuatu. Thus, it makes sense that people would be interested in an Ura–Sye or an Ura–Bislama dictionary.

However, in order to find a respectable publisher for a dictionary of Ura from whom I will earn appropriate 'research quantum', it would need to be an Ura–English dictionary. But an entry that translates the Ura word *lau* as 'heliconia' is unlikely to be particularly illuminating to most Erromangans. The simple fact is that most Erromangans have only six years (or less) of primary education, and I very much doubt that the English word *heliconia* is at all widely known. (In fact, how many native speakers of English know what a heliconia is?) On the other hand, if I were to gloss Ura *lau* as *ndau* in Syc, everybody on the island—of whatever level of education in English—would know immediately what it means. Given that Bislama is the national language, translating Ura *lau* as Bislama *lif laplap* would also be immediately and universally understood.

While an Ura–Sye dictionary would satisfy local needs, I would almost certainly not be able to find a respectable academic publisher to produce such a volume. There would be only 1,900 potential buyers in the world, all living on the island of Erromango, and most of those people could not afford to buy such a volume anyway, as they are living a largely subsistence lifestyle. An Ura–Bislama dictionary would also fail to attract orders from libraries overseas on which many small specialist publishers depend for sales.

Finally, I was well aware that Erromangans badly wanted to see me produce a dictionary of their Sye language. People seemed to compete with each other to think of new words and expressions with obscure meanings for me to include in my dictionary. I could not go anywhere without people asking me if I had recorded the word for things such as little toe, haemorrhoid, or a particular kind of soil that is only found in caves (with a high content of bat droppings) which causes the skin to itch if you get it on yourself. Older people were also keen to ply me with words that younger people generally do not know, and which they would like to see recorded for posterity. Some older people also asked me to ensure that certain words should be recorded only with their 'correct' original meanings, rather than the innovative 'incorrect' meanings that are encountered in the speech of younger people.

In the end, I did produce my grammars (Crowley 1998*b*, 1999: 106–225), and I also produced my Sye–English and Ura–English dictionaries (Crowley 1999: 10–69, 2000), and I dutifully deposited copies of all of these materials in the national archive. However, while I was happy to return copies of the dictionaries to the local community—along with a printed collection of stories, as I will discuss below—I have never been able to bring myself to give people copies of the grammars that I wrote, let alone even to show them to people on the island. I am overwhelmingly confident that the sections headed Morphophonemics, Subordinate Clauses, and Counterassertive Verbal Paradigms—in fact, just about the whole thing—would be completely unintelligible to just about everybody.

2.2.2 Dictionaries

Clearly, then, producing a dictionary of a language is part of the solution to this ethical dilemma. It is particularly disappointing to note, however, that while sometimes even the most eminent of descriptive linguists may put considerable effort into producing published grammars which are widely distributed among the academic community, they make no attempt to publish extensive dictionaries or text compilations which may well be of considerably greater interest to local communities. Part of our task as field linguists, then, should be to put pressure on any ethically delinquent linguist who produces only a grammatical description of a language and who fails to follow this up with a published dictionary, or some other body of material that is accessible to, and appreciated in some way by, the local community.

But doing the right thing by a community is not as straightforward as simply deciding to write a dictionary. In my experience, the kinds of dictionaries that have been produced by linguists in the past have, by and large, *not* been nearly as accessible as they could be to speakers of the languages that are represented in them. Some of the faults which typically lie with these dictionaries include the following:

   (i) Dictionaries are typically produced bilingually with definitions given in the linguist's language. This will typically be a major world language, which is more than likely going to be English. Many speakers will not know enough of the major language to be able to gain anything from the definition, especially as many meanings will need to be defined using fairly difficult terminology, as I have already illustrated with respect to a definition of Ura *lau* as 'heliconia'.

   (ii) Dictionaries often contain a lot of distracting information which may require a considerable amount of effort or education—and sometimes even technical training in linguistics—to decipher. For instance, Keesing's (1975: 155) dictionary of the Kwaio language of the Solomon Islands includes a definition such as the following (set out as indicated):

2478 mooli 2.
*mauli *ML
mooli differently, a different way, in a wrong direction

I invite you to imagine what this must look like to an uneducated speaker of Kwaio, who will typically be bilingual only in Kwaio and Pijin, the national lingua franca. Precisely why it was thought necessary, for example, to indicate that this was the 2,478th entry in the dictionary is beyond me.

(iii) Forms are often cited in non-occurring underlying roots rather than widely used citation forms encountered in natural speech. Thus, Crowley (1978: 213) cites the verb /wadʲi/ 'tell' in the Bandjalang language of New South Wales in its underlying form, despite the fact that it only ever appears in inflected forms such as the following (some of which involve a systematic lowering in the final vowel of the root when lengthening is involved): /wadʲini/ 'told', /wadʲiya:/ 'in order to tell', /wadʲe:ɲ/ 'will tell', /wadʲe:/ 'tell' (imperative).

(iv) Many dictionaries are produced by publishers who need to keep costs to a minimum, so there is little sophistication in terms of the creative use of font, illustrations, and layout. Newly literate dictionary users are often faced by typographically fairly uniform pages with no illustrations, and little use of indentation and white space. The pages are, quite simply, daunting. There are enough publications of this type that it would be unfair to refer to a single author's work as an example.

(v) Dictionaries are often presented in some version of a phonemic script rather than a more recognizable spelling system. Crowley (1978) is guilty of this for Bandjalang (along with many others with regard to other languages). In the spelling that is preferred by the local community, /wadʲe:ɲ/ 'will tell' is written *wadhehyn*, with /dʲ/ being represented by *dh*, vowel length by *h*, and word-final /ɲ/ by *yn*.

(vi) Dictionaries are too expensive and difficult for individuals to order in remote rural communities where people often live substantially

according to a subsistence lifestyle. Linguistics publications typically cost many times more than what most people pay for the only
other book in their possession, such as the Bible and hymnals.
While these religious materials are usually easily obtainable
locally, the only way to obtain other published books is to obtain
a bank draft in foreign currency to order overseas, which in most
remote locations is simply not practical.

In Crowley (1992), I attempted to overcome some—though by no
means all—of these problems in my published dictionary of Paamese.
In particular, I put some of the distracting linguistic information, such as
underlying forms of roots, towards the end of an entry, with the entry
itself being cited under the least marked inflected form. Thus, for
example, the word for 'eye' was entered as *meten*, which means 'his/her/
its eye', rather than the underlying root *mete-* which never appears as such
in isolation. The verb meaning 'fat' is entered as *raho*, which means '(s)he/
it is/was fat', rather than under the underlying root *tahoo*.

However, I also set out to produce a dictionary that would earn me
some academic brownie points, in that I intended it to include information
that academic linguists could make use of. Because I had attempted to
compromise—albeit only partially—in the direction of community interests, this meant that it was necessarily going to involve a bit more work
on the part of academic linguists to find some of the kinds of information
that they are traditionally accustomed to being given on a plate.

An academic who goes too far in making his/her dictionary accessible
to a local community runs the risk of attracting criticism from his/her
fellow academics, i.e. you start losing brownie points. One reviewer of my
dictionary clearly recognized that it was intended to be more accessible to
the local community than many other dictionaries when he commented,
'[Crowley] aimed this [work on Paamese] at a different audience'
(Bradshaw 1994: 262). However, the reviewer also went on to say, 'But
I do regret that the dictionary is of such limited utility to linguists' (ibid.)
and he commented further that, '[T]he traditional audience of...
linguists will find this dictionary almost as frustrating to use as non-
linguist speakers of the relevant languages will find the other 120 books
[of Pacific Linguistics]' (Bradshaw 1994: 257). The very points that made
the dictionary relatively accessible to speakers of Paamese were, by and
large, the ones that the reviewer then spent a significant proportion of the

remainder of the review criticizing. It seems, then, that an ethically responsive lexicographer cannot easily win.

Different linguistic situations in the world would call for different kinds of appropriate lexicographical responses. I have for the most part been discussing situations where a language is actively spoken by a community that makes little use of a major world language such as English as part of its normal repertoire with in-group members. In many parts of Aboriginal Australia, as well as in New Zealand, and also in Canada and the United States, indigenous people often no longer speak traditional languages natively, having switched largely to some variety of English. The lexicographical needs of such people are going to be more similar to those of the language learner than of the native speaker, so their dictionaries will necessarily be bilingual. However, they will still need to be stripped of purely linguistic distractions. Some community-friendly work of this kind has been produced in recent years by academic linguists, though much valuable lexicographical information still lies to a large extent semi-hidden from community view by a strict adherence to academic conventions.

A dictionary of a moribund language that is intended to be community-friendly would possibly need to be more prescriptive than a dictionary that is prepared with native speakers in mind because users would not have the benefit of native-speaker intuitions to fall back on in their interpretation of material in entries. Thus, for languages that have large native-speaker populations, a certain amount of phonological ambiguity might be acceptable in a dictionary, with, for example, contrastive vowel length perhaps not being marked. In the case of Maori in New Zealand, only about 10 per cent of the total Maori population are native speakers of the language. This means that the majority of dictionary users are now likely to be non-native speakers learning the language in a classroom situation. In this case, the unambiguous marking of vowel length becomes essential.

There is also likely to be a much greater need for illustrative sentences in such a dictionary than would be required of a dictionary aimed at native speakers. If a word is identified for its word class membership, it could be assumed that native speakers will be able correctly to use that word if the classification of word classes is sufficiently finely tuned. However, when the users of a dictionary are predominantly non-native speakers, the presentation of the form in an illustrative sentence (or two) could be extremely helpful, and perhaps even essential.

Western linguists need to ask this fundamental question when working on other languages: What kinds of dictionaries *should* be produced for minority languages? In an ideal world, perhaps we should aim to produce two different dictionaries for every language, i.e. a linguist-friendly volume and a separate community-friendly volume. With computer technology, the same database could be adapted to these different formats without too much additional work, though the community-friendly dictionaries would still need both a generous benefactor to finance their production, as well as an academic who is willing to devote some of his or her precious research time to this task for minimal academic reward. By depositing the digital database in a suitable repository you will be providing a useful basis for others to rework the data, perhaps to construct other kinds of dictionaries, perhaps to use in lists of lexical comparisons.

Given the likelihood that these goals will probably only be easily achievable for a relatively small number of languages, we should probably aim to produce volumes that are going to be reasonably acceptable to both audiences. Some academic dictionary users will therefore need to accept that features of future dictionaries might present them with some level of inconvenience. This might include the citation of inflected forms of obligatorily bound roots rather than underlying uninflected roots. It will also mean more work for lexicographers in that it may be necessary to negotiate with a community regarding which particular inflected form should be adopted as the citation form in cases where there is no immediately obvious candidate. Lexicographers will also need to make more creative use of font and layout choices, as well as illustrations. The fact that many dictionaries have in the past been produced in IPA script effectively renders them of little value to community members. Lexicographers should show themselves to be more willing to provide entries in a carefully considered practical orthography that is acceptable to a community, with a clear guide for linguists as to how this should be interpreted in phonemic terms.

If a dictionary is to be published bilingually, then the English–Vernacular section should ideally be much more than a simple reversal of the Vernacular–English section, so that learners of English can look for definitions of unfamiliar English words in the language that they know best. This would again require more work from lexicographers, as they would have to come up with useful vernacular definitions of words such as *codicil* (and many more) which do not appear in the list of translation equivalents in the Vernacular–English section. Ideally, they would need to translate all of the definitions in, say, the *Oxford Advanced Learner's Dictionary* into the language. In reality, of course, they would need to decide which additional English words can be most practically included in the English–Vernacular section beyond the simple reversal.

This is essentially the kind of model that I followed in the production of a recent dictionary of Bislama (Crowley 1995). Despite the fact that I consciously adopted practices that I felt would be received positively by non-linguists who speak both Bislama and English, it is a dictionary from which I think a considerable amount of useful information can still be extracted by academic linguists. At the same time, it was hard work to produce that dictionary for me, and it was a task that I have felt unable to replicate in my published dictionaries of other smaller vernaculars.

There is one kind of dictionary that would be unambiguously aimed at speakers of the language rather than members of the academic community and that would be a monolingual dictionary, in which words are defined in that language itself, rather than simply being given translation equivalents in a major world language. However, such a dictionary would normally be such a major task that it would be well beyond the capabilities of the individual researcher, so this would not represent a practical solution to the ordinary fieldworker's ethical pressure to produce useful and valuable materials for the community. In addition to the size of the task, there is also a question of economics. The production of a monolingual dictionary might be financially viable for a language with a relatively large number of speakers, as long as a substantial proportion of the population has enough buying power, and as long as the language in question has a confirmed place within the education system of the country. Even so, it is likely that such a task would be impractical without a considerable amount of funding support, and the amount of work involved would call for a well-coordinated team of lexicographers working together for many years.

This is never likely to be a practical proposition for many of the smallest languages of the world. However, it might still be possible to meet conflicting demands by adopting a 'mono-bilingual' approach, i.e. by providing bilingual glosses (combined with a comprehensive English–Vernacular section), as well as monolingual definitions. This would result in a certain amount of typographic clutter and it would be necessary to find ways to clearly distinguish material in different languages to make such a dictionary usable to its two audiences.

2.2.3 Reading materials

Another obvious contribution that a researcher can make is to produce some kind of community materials that will feed into community interests in promoting vernacular literacy. It would therefore represent a valid contribution alongside your grammar to respond to a request first to help in the development of a spelling system that is acceptable to the community, and also to help in the production of reading materials which make use of that spelling system.

With regard to the development of a writing system, many of us learn very early on in our linguistic training that the ideal spelling system for a language is one which matches each distinct phoneme in the language with a unique orthographic symbol or, when no appropriate single-symbol spelling is apparent, perhaps making use of a digraph or a diacritic. In sticking rigidly to this requirement, many of us seem to forget that a spelling system which falls short of this idea can still be perfectly serviceable. Witness, for example, the perfectly readable horrors of the spelling system of the language in which I am writing right now. What is more important for a spelling system than its strict adherence to the phonemic principle is systematic usage and community acceptability. It may well be that a community is going to be perfectly happy to use a spelling system which fails to mark certain phonemic contrasts.

For example, in the Paamese language of Vanuatu, there is a phonemic contrast between long and short vowels. This is not a contrast that is found in just a handful of words either. It has very high functional load, with lots and lots of minimal pairs. The Paamese have been writing their language for about a century now using a spelling system that was originally devised by Presbyterian missionaries who had never heard of phonemes. In that spelling system, short and long vowels were represented identically, yet this does not seem to cause any problems for speakers of the language. They seem to be able to work out which vowels are to be pronounced long and which are short from the context in which the word appears. A linguist would be taking a great risk in a situation such as this in producing a collection of reading materials intended for community use in which a revision to the spelling system is foisted upon the community, at least without some kind of process of consultation with and acceptance from the community.

There are also cases of spelling systems which do make all of the phonemic contrasts but do so in a way which may not appeal to the linguist for some reason. I can think of another language where there is a phonemic contrast of vowel length where the tradition in the community has been to mark the long vowels with macrons (or not to mark length at all). A linguist working on this language produced a very substantial dictionary in which long vowels were written instead as double vowels, i.e. *aa*, *ee*, *ii*, etc. When this dictionary appeared, people in the community wanted nothing to do with it even though otherwise it was an excellent piece of work.

So, a linguist needs to learn some humility when it comes to proposing a spelling system for a language. You may think that a certain orthographic solution is particularly elegant, but you must be prepared for the possibility that you may not be able to sell your idea to the community. For instance, I have been involved in the preparation of reading materials and a dictionary for the Neveʻei language of Vanuatu. In this language, there is a contrast between ordinary bilabial consonants and labio-velar consonants. This contrast is also found in Paamese, and the established tradition there is to write the labio-velars with a tilde, e.g. m̃, ṽ. This is a practice that is fairly common in other languages of Vanuatu where the same contrast is made.

I therefore suggested to Neveʻei speakers that they could represent their labio-velars in the same way, and they initially agreed. I went ahead and produced a substantial collection of draft reading materials based on transcriptions of recorded stories, as well as a draft dictionary. I sent this back to members of the community to look at. On my next visit, people were asking me what the strange wiggly thing was in the materials that I had written. It seems that even though they had agreed that this was a reasonable way to write these sounds, they were not familiar with the use of this symbol in other languages, and they were not able to work out how I had used it for theirs.

So, I had to sit down once more with people and come up with a better solution. It seemed that they were far happier in the end using digraphs, and opted instead for the spellings *mw*, *vw*. Fortunately, computers make it relatively easy to effect such changes with the 'change-all' command, and I sent out a completely revised version of the earlier materials.

When I went back to the village the next time, there was not a single comment along the lines of: What's that strange *w* in these materials? That led me to assume that perhaps people were much more satisfied with the new spellings that I had used for their language.

If a community wants to initiate some kind of initial vernacular programme for their children, they may legitimately expect you to help in the production of appropriate reading materials which goes beyond assistance with the development of a spelling system. You may feel that this is outside your area of expertise, but you can always seek the advice of others who do have such expertise if you are not confident. If there are members of the Summer Institute of Linguistics active locally, they will often respond positively with advice when they can.

This kind of assistance need not represent a major drain on your time or energy, especially if the community is enthusiastic about the project. In the village of Vinmavis in Vanuatu, for example, a church-run school wanted to encourage its children to begin reading in their own language rather than through the medium of English, which none of the young children could speak, or even understand. A teacher at another school had already produced a series of Big Book readers aimed at pre-school children. The text was handwritten in Bislama, and each line of text had a page-sized colour illustration that teachers and other community members had drawn themselves. The decision was taken to translate the text of these stories into the local Neve'ei language in association with the same illustrations. None of the stories was more than half a dozen lines long, and translating the text of a few dozen stories into Neve'ei did not take more than a day when I sat down to work with a couple of the teachers.

I was then able electronically to scan each of the illustrations, and I typed in the relevant line of text beneath it in a large clear font. The pages were printed in colour, spiral-bound, and provided with a clear plastic cover at low cost. For relatively little effort, as well as limited cost, the community now has a collection of vernacular stories which, for the first time, will allow pre-school teachers to read stories to their children in their own language. If the books are damaged or lost, I can easily produce a new printout and send it off to the community. Having seen these Big Books, members of the community will see how easy it would be to produce more of the same, and it will not be difficult for me to help in their production if that is what the community wants.

Another contribution that you may be called upon to make is the provision of written forms of any oral tradition that you may have recorded as the basis for your grammatical study. This is something that communities may well see as very important, because the older traditions of passing down stories are often being eroded. This is also something that you can provide which will not be too difficult for you to do.

While this may seem like a relatively straightforward process, there are still some significant issues that you will need to pay attention to. First, simply copying your transcriptions, even if presented in a practical orthography, is unlikely to represent a satisfactory response to a community's expectations. If your transcriptions accurately reflect the way that somebody has spoken, unless a storyteller has remarkable narrative skills, then it is likely that they will contain a number of different kinds of performance errors which people will be most unhappy about seeing recorded in writing in perpetuity.

This will involve the local equivalent of *ums* and *ahs*, which are the easiest elements of all to edit out. However, there are other performance issues which you will need to be aware of. People sometimes accidentally give a character's name wrongly, or mention an incorrect place where something happened. While this may seem unimportant to you, it can sometimes be of great importance locally, as all sorts of other things may follow from the story that you are unaware of. For example, a story may provide some kind of justification for one group's ownership of a particular area of land, in which case it is obviously going to be of considerable importance to ensure that the details are recorded correctly in a written form of a story that is going to be distributed publicly.

Sometimes when telling a story, people skip ahead to a point that has not yet been mentioned and then they backtrack to the original point in the story. Sometimes also, the narrator may say something like *He said such-and-such* and *He did this*, without clearly signalling which character in the story is talking and which character is performing a particular action. Often, because local people are already familiar to some extent with the content of the story, this does not cause any confusion. In any case, there will often be some kind of subtle clues as to what's going on in the narrator's intonation or the facial expression, rather than in the words. However, when you are converting a written transcription into a written text, local people may feel that it is necessary to reorganize certain elements of the story as it was told, and to insert additional clues clearly to indicate who is saying and doing what. This is something that you can't always do by yourself, so you will need to have local editorial help in converting your transcriptions into acceptable written texts.

2.2.4 Technical advice

A linguist's input into a community need not just take the form of published outputs. Given the lack of trained linguists in many Pacific countries, one legitimate activity that we can engage in is the provision of technical advice to governments and other agencies in these countries (Bradley 1998: 52). Such advice could then be taken into account in the formulation of social policies, whether implemented by government or non-government organizations. There is a wide range of published material already available relating to choices which are available for different countries, and linguists could provide their personal perspectives on these materials in relation to individual countries on the basis of their own field experience.

It must also be recognized that attention is most likely to be paid to such advice when it is given in response to a local request rather than when it is simply offered by an academic (or, as sometimes happens, when it is effectively thrust upon a local audience). Local people all around the world have had to develop strategies for listening to the advice of overseas 'experts' who sometimes spend only a week or two in the country before depositing their wisdom and then leaving (while drawing upon often quite hefty consultancy fees). Such advice is not infrequently politely received and then—sometimes quite justifiably—ignored in large part, or even in total. Effective action can only come from internally motivated policies, rather than those imposed from outside (Ostler 1998).

2.2.5 Public awareness

Public awareness of the current linguistic situation in a country is an essential element in any plan for concerted action regarding language maintenance. Kaplan and Baldauf (2002: 222–5) discuss prestige planning as one of four major types of language planning activity, alongside status planning, corpus planning, and language-in-education planning. Professional linguists clearly have a legitimate role to play in making people aware of what has happened in comparable situations in other countries, and what kinds of activities have proved useful—or less than useful—in those countries.

Education of this kind can be provided through local tertiary institutions and the various national teacher training institutions, as well as a range of non-government organizations, and the national and regional media organizations. Linguists could also make use of their own social networks in the countries where they have worked to provide local people with knowledge about what is already happening regarding the status and use of local languages, as well as reasonable and viable ways of acting against any negative trends.

Closely related to the issue of public awareness, of course, is the question of community motivation. It is arguably not enough simply to make people aware of issues relating to language maintenance, as language communities need to be encouraged to feel confident in their own ability to stand up against globalizing socio-economic and cultural pressures which serve to threaten the future viability of minority languages. The kind of action of this kind that could be practicably performed by a linguist would be making people aware not only of the dangers facing a language on the basis of experience elsewhere in the world, but also making people aware of some of the successes that communities have enjoyed in maintaining their languages against external threats.

Much useful work in the area of public awareness is fortunately already being done, though arguably only a small proportion of those whose opinions need to be influenced have been successfully reached in this way. Tertiary institutions have a capability to re-educate influential people in policy-making positions, though in my experience the shortage of such well-educated people, combined with the political instability of many newly independent countries, means that there is often little guarantee that a positive-thinking individual will necessarily be in the same area of responsibility in a year's time.

The activities to which I have just referred essentially represent a top-down approach in which the effects of awareness programmes are expected to trickle down to the community at large from people placed in positions of responsibility, most probably in the public sector. However, public awareness can also be promoted via a bottom-up approach in which emphasis is placed on raising awareness at the local level. Faraclas (1996), for example, discusses the promotion of vernacular literacy in the context of a programme of more general language awareness in Papua New Guinea. However, individuals and non-government organizations can often provide influence only on a small scale at a local level because of funding limitations or a restricted infrastructure. In any case, it would be very difficult for a professional linguist to have any substantial input into language programmes beyond a very restricted geographical area with which they are familiar.

2.2.6 Terminology development

It is rather more difficult for a linguist to provide answers to the perennial question of how speakers of a Pacific language might express introduced concepts without using borrowed vocabulary. Some descriptive linguists are loath to regard borrowings as necessarily bad, though it must be acknowledged that there is a widespread implicit tendency even among linguists to view borrowings prescriptively as suspect.

A linguist can obviously make suggestions to speakers of a particular language as to how a new meaning might be expressed based on what he or she knows of how such issues have been resolved in other language groups, whether as a result of spontaneous linguistic development or conscious language planning. Amery (pers. comm.) reports that a base-ten counting system has been created for the Kaurna language of South Australia—for which there was originally no counting system—out of the roots of a no longer used series of birth-order names for children.

However, the question of whether a 'plane' should be expressed in a particular language by simply borrowing the word from English (as, say, *plen*), by extending the meaning of an existing word (such as Paamese *aman* 'bird'), or by joining together two existing indigenous roots to make a new word (such as Fijian *waqa-vuka* 'boat-fly') is going to depend entirely on local community preferences. Once again, therefore, the input of a linguist is likely to be restricted, with the final outcome being decided on the basis of community preferences.

2.2.7 Recognizing our limitations

Beyond these areas of activity, however, it is difficult in many cases to imagine what more any individual linguist could possibly be expected to achieve with regard to language maintenance, apart, perhaps, from the very limited degree of language revival that has been reported in situations such as that to which I referred earlier for Kaurna. There are certainly other areas of activity which can be considered as possibly contributing to language maintenance, such as the incorporation of vernaculars into the education systems, or the promotion of opportunities for social and economic advancement without the need for urbanization or overseas (or internal) migration. However, actions in these areas are clearly matters which lie outside the purview of professional linguists, and are for the most part beyond the influence of any single individual.

We no longer live in a world where outsiders can come into a recently independent country and tell people what they must do, how they must speak, or even what language they must (or must not) use. The ultimate choices are now up to speakers of local languages themselves. If they make choices which lead ultimately to the loss of their own languages, our responsibility as linguists can only extend to making people aware of what the related issues are, and what are the various options that might be available along the way.

Such an attitude may suggest that I am being dispassionate about the possible loss of indigenous languages. However, I know of no linguist who doesn't experience considerable angst at the loss—or imminent loss—of a language. I have been a close witness to more examples of this phenomenon than I care to contemplate. While I do not find this loss any easier to accept with each new situation that I encounter, I recognize that it would be presumptuous of me to try to dictate to people how and when they should speak their own languages.

It must also be recognized that a linguist's sense of loss does not necessarily always match up with what members of a local community are feeling. In the case of Ura, for example, it would be fair to say that people are mildly sad at most that the language is moribund, and Lynch (1998: 270–1) indicates that speakers of other vernaculars in the Pacific have even enthusiastically embarked on a path of language shift. Attempting to preach against language shift in these kinds of situations would be akin to a situation where a linguist who drinks Coca-Cola tries to tell other people that Coca-Cola is bad for them and they should refuse to drink it, restricting themselves to drinking only fresh coconuts.

Another disconcerting trend that faces many academic linguists is the fact that market forces now dominate in tertiary education in the western world, with an increasing tendency towards the commodification of courses—and even research—in contrast to the older emphasis on tertiary education primarily for the sake of learning in its own right. Many of us feel these days that we are teaching at the University of Bums-on-Seats.

Given that there are still several thousand languages in the world awaiting documentation—and a substantial number of these are under varying degrees of threat—it would take several thousand additional linguists quite a few years of their academic careers to carry out this task. It seems unlikely that university administrations and funding agencies world wide will commit their shrinking resources towards funding such a large-scale enterprise, when even holding onto existing teaching positions in academic institutions in linguistics these days is enough of a challenge.

Traditional linguistic analysis is therefore not nearly as 'sexy' as it once was among vice chancellors and deans as more and more people are being tempted by the money-earning potential of a qualification in English-teaching. Linguistics, after having concentrated since Sapir's time on describing a wide variety of small and previously undocumented languages, is in serious danger of being recolonized by specialists in English (or other major languages), to the exclusion of minor or threatened languages.

2.3 Linguists and other linguists

The final ethical guidelines that we should keep in mind relate to our relationships with our colleagues. I am not talking just about standard issues such as the proper acknowledgement of other people's work, the avoidance of plagiarism, the need to be sure that we have accurately reflected somebody's views when we discuss their work in print, or the need to avoid the falsification of our data. Rather, I want to concentrate specifically on fieldwork-related behaviour.

First, given that there are so many undocumented languages out there, the field does not need to be a crowded place. Some linguists have a tendency occasionally to be a little territorial and do not like to feel that other researchers are getting too close to their fieldwork area. Rather than viewing somebody who is working in a language close to where we are working ourselves as a threat, we should of course welcome the opportunity for more data to be made public from a nearby language.

At the same time, in choosing your own fieldwork site, you need to be aware of people's possible sensitivities. This means that you should consult ahead of time with people who know an area to make sure that you are not going to end up stepping on somebody else's toes with your project. I can think of one case where a linguist had been working on one language for some time, and there were several small languages spoken nearby which she might also ultimately have taken the opportunity to gather data on. However, another linguist then arrived, began gathering data, and only when his work was well under way did he ask, 'You don't have any problem with me working on these languages, do you?' That could be seen as rather like a smoker lighting a cigarette and then saying, 'You don't mind if I smoke, do you?' It would have been so much more considerate not to have presented the other person with the fait accompli in the first place.

It particularly makes no sense to plan on describing a language that somebody else already has plans to work on, or that they have started work on but have not yet had an opportunity to complete their work. In such cases, you should graciously shift your attention to another field site, as there are bound to be plenty of other opportunities, unless your intention is to work on the language from a substantially different perspective from that of the original researcher.

Any field linguist should regard it as a duty to make his or her data publicly available in some kind of publication. Publication means that your data can be seen and easily cited by others. This means that a grammatical description and an accompanying dictionary for the language you have been working on should be published. Primary data (field recordings, transcripts, texts, and the lexical database that is the source for the published dictionary) should be deposited with a linguistic archive. It can be very frustrating to see a draft copy of somebody's work that comes with warnings that the work is preliminary and that it should not be cited, but where the final work never appears. I know of far too many cases where people have worked on languages for many years—sometimes even decades—and they have never produced a grammar in a form that can be publicly cited. Of course, sometimes circumstances may prevent an individual from publishing a linguistic description. In such cases, linguists should be prepared to provide copies to other interested people.

Keeping one's data to oneself is not just selfish; it is also risky. If your unpublished work has been deposited in a professionally curated archive, it may be relatively safe. I have heard of far too many cases where the only copy of a potentially valuable set of data has been lost in cyclones, fires, volcanic eruptions, earthquakes, or where data has simply been mislaid. The last speaker of the Utaha language of Erromango died in 1954. His language was almost completely undocumented, so before he died, he apparently wrote down quite a lot of material in some notebooks. However, nobody now knows where those notebooks are. The linguistic material that was lost in those notes was completely irreplaceable.

As a final point regarding the storage of data, you may find that your Ethics Committee has established a generic guideline that primary data should be destroyed after a given period. When people in a variety of social sciences are conducting surveys and interviews, it is essential that the data be available to the researcher while the analysis and write-up is proceeding. The data must also be available for some time after that so that any challenges to publications arising out of this data can be met. However, some committees prefer to see primary data destroyed after a given period as a way of guaranteeing the privacy of the various participants.

When faced with this prospect in relation to ethical approval for one of my linguistic projects, I was able to persuade the relevant committee that in the discipline of linguistics it would be the destruction of primary data that would be unethical rather than its non-destruction. Speakers of languages typically agree to participate in projects of linguistic documentation precisely so that the data that they provide *will* be available in perpetuity, especially if their language is one that is likely to disappear with the passing of the current generation of speakers. We cannot hope to extract every single piece of useful information from our recordings, as we cannot always foresee what sorts of questions people will be asking about language data in the distant future. If, in 200 years' time, all of the relatively small number of languages in which there are bilabial trills have become extinct and I failed to keep my recordings of the Avava language of Vanuatu in which such sounds are quite common, my foolishness would rightly be condemned by future generations of linguists.

I have been talking about the role of academic linguists in the promotion of indigenous languages so far on the assumption that the linguists in question are expatriates, and for the most part Europeans. This is in fact true in large part in many parts of the world. From time to time, one hears arguments about the lack of influence of speakers of indigenous languages in descriptive linguistics, usually in private conversations, at conferences and seminar presentations, or in email discussion forums (though relatively rarely in published form). Some such commentary engenders spirited debate, as it is very often formulated in terms of white western academics consciously or subconsciously excluding indigenous linguists from working on their own languages. In such forums, linguistics is effectively painted as a neo-colonial discipline (though it should be acknowledged that there are relatively few areas of social science research where the same would not be true).

In reply, it can be pointed out that some conference organizers go to great lengths to attempt to include native-speaker linguists in their conference programmes. In some cases, the native-speaker linguists who participate do so on a completely equal basis with other linguists, all sharing the same kinds of descriptive and theoretical interests (such as has happened recently with the series of Austronesian Formal Linguistics Association conferences). However, in order to maximize the participation of speakers of Pacific languages in linguistic conferences, it has usually proved necessary to include specially designed sections of the conference relating to applied issues (such as happened, for example, at the Fourth International Conference in Oceanic Linguistics held in Niue in the Pacific in 1999), or to organize completely separate conferences exclusively around applied themes, to which descriptive and theoretical linguists are either not invited, or in which it is accepted that they will have minimal interest (such as with the Pacific Languages: Directions for the Future conference held in Vanuatu in 1984, the Vernacular Languages in South Pacific Education conference held in Vanuatu in 1988, or UNESCO-sponsored conferences held in Papua New Guinea in 1999 and in Fiji in 2001).

A straightforward insistence that conferences on descriptive or theoretical (or historical) linguistics *must* be attended by native speakers can turn out to be as patronizing as any assumption that native speakers should not be present, if those people happen to have primarily applied interests. Those in attendance are likely to be either bored or confounded by the theoretical presentations, and nobody is likely to benefit from the attendance of native speakers.

There is, however, a rather more objectionable assumption which is implicit in this kind of argument, and that is the idea that there is something inherently more worthy about descriptive, theoretical, and historical work in linguistics over linguistics in the Pacific that is applied to language maintenance issues. This kind of thinking is surely just as patronizing as that which seeks to exclude speakers of local languages from less applied forums. Linguistics as a discipline therefore needs to accord greater recognition to the value of applied—as against purely theoretical and descriptive—activities in order for the contributions of indigenous linguists to be fully recognized. In this regard, then, Dixon's (2001) view that the only worthy linguist is one who has produced a full descriptive account of a language must be resisted by emphasizing the validity of a wide range of different kinds of linguistics.

Keeping in mind that in many parts of the world, there are still relatively few—if any—speakers of indigenous languages who are formally qualified to practise as linguists, an outsider-linguist should as far as possible seek to involve any qualified insiders within our projects, and to plan genuine research partnerships leading to jointly authored publications. I am aware of one case where somebody with a postgraduate qualification in linguistics who is a native speaker of a moribund language had an interest in doing descriptive work on that language. However, an outsider linguist happened along and effectively pulled the rug from beneath their feet by independently gathering a lot of data, doing all of the analysis, and gaining sole authorship of the resulting publication, leaving the indigenous linguist feeling rather let down. This kind of behaviour is something that we should all seek to avoid.

Further reading: Dwyer (2006), Rice (2005).

3
Getting Started

3.1 The fieldworker

In its simplest terms, linguistic fieldwork involves a language, somebody who speaks the language, and you, the fieldworker. Some linguists are drawn to fieldwork, and I am one of those. Right from when I started my undergraduate programme in linguistics, I was fascinated by stories of linguistic discoveries involving previously undocumented languages.

I was lucky enough to be sent on my first fieldtrip at the end of my second year of undergraduate study. Linguistically speaking, it wasn't a very productive trip. I had been sent to Tasmania to record what little was still remembered of the original Aboriginal languages of the island, which certainly was not much. But it was nevertheless exciting to try to relate what I had recorded with what had already been documented. I was hooked, and since that time, I have probably carried out some kind of fieldwork every year.

Other linguists seem to regard a stint of fieldwork as something like a rite of passage. It is something they endure—and possibly, to an extent at least, even enjoy—early in their career. When they have served their time, they then retire to the comfort of their office for the remainder of their tenure. Yet other linguists, while recognizing the importance of fieldwork, express puzzlement as to why sane academics would willingly submit themselves to all manner of discomfort, and possibly even danger, by disappearing into the bush for months on end to study a language.

Of course, every linguist has something to offer the discipline. If you are one of those who shudders at the very thought of a day-long hike across a tropical island with a heavy pack on your back, or hanging over the rail of an ocean-going vessel while you feed the marlin, then we will all be better off if you stay where you are. It is almost impossible to generalize about what sort of person will make a good fieldworker and what sort of person will not. While there are certainly some linguists I have met who I would never want to inflict on any community, people with a wide diversity of personality types have succeeded at fieldwork in the past. I have known successful fieldworkers who are extroverted and introverted; boorish and boring; technophile and technophobic; young and old; male and female; single and married; religious and non-religious; heterosexual, homosexual, bisexual, and asexual.

What you *do* need is solid training in all of the main areas of descriptive linguistics: articulatory phonetics, phonology, morphology, and syntax. A knowledge of cross-cultural communication and lexicography is also helpful, though many people seem to be able to pick up what is needed once they get going. But in addition to all of this, you need to have a burning desire to do fieldwork.

3.2 Choosing a language

You, as a potential linguistic fieldworker, will need to make your own decision about which language family you are going to work in. A wide variety of considerations are likely to come into play when you make this kind of decision. You may have an interest in particular kinds of languages (tone languages, languages with bilabial trills, languages with free word order, ergative languages, languages with serial verbs, object-incorporating languages) or languages of a particular geographical area (Papuan languages, South-East Asian languages, West African languages, Amerindian languages) or languages from a particular genetic grouping (Australian languages, Austronesian languages, Mon-Khmer languages).

Since successful fieldwork will in many cases call for an advanced command of a language other than English—French in many parts of Africa, Portuguese in Brazil, Spanish in Central and most of South America, Bahasa Indonesia in Indonesia, Melanesian Pidgin in Papua New Guinea, Solomon Islands, and Vanuatu, Mandarin in China, Hindi in many parts of India, Russian in Russia, and so on—you may also be guided in your ultimate destination by your current language capabilities. If you have an excellent command of French but you know no Spanish, it probably makes more sense to look for a field site in francophone Africa rather than Mexico.

Unless personal factors come into play in determining which particular language community you are going to try to work in—maybe you have close friends from a particular place, maybe you are married to somebody who speaks a particular language, maybe there is a fantastic surf beach that you want to be based near—then you are going to have to make some decisions about your preferred specific destination. You may be lucky enough to have taken a specialist linguistics course in the languages of a particular area or a particular language family which will give you some of the background information that you need to help you to zero in on a suitable field site. Alternatively, you may be attracted to a field site as a result of contact with a language during a linguistic field methods course in your undergraduate years.

If you haven't made any decisions about where to go, then the first thing you need to do is some background reading. These days, there are increasing numbers of survey volumes produced by major publishing houses that provide excellent overviews of particular groupings of languages. Surveys of this type typically include up-to-date and detailed lists of additional sources. Curzon Press, for example, has survey volumes in print—or at least planned—in its Curzon Language Family Series on the Oceanic languages, the Austronesian languages of Asia and Madagascar, the Khoesan languages, the Manchu-Tungusic languages, the Sino-Tibetan languages, the Indo-Aryan languages, the Iranian languages, the languages of the Caucasus, the Bantu languages, and the Mongolic languages. Cambridge University Press also has survey volumes in its Cambridge Language Surveys series on Australian languages, Dravidian languages, Indo-Aryan languages, North American languages, and Papuan languages. Routledge have produced—or are planning—a number of volumes in their Routledge Language Family Series, including surveys of Bantu languages, Indo-Aryan languages, Mongolic languages, and Oceanic languages. With just these publishers, a substantial proportion of the world's language groupings are represented, and a little careful searching in library catalogues or on the internet should fairly quickly enable you to fill any gaps.

These volumes will typically provide quite a deal of information about the language family as a whole. It is important to get some idea of the kinds of features that are widely distributed in the languages of the family that you are planning to work in. This can save you from having to reinvent the wheel if other people have successfully tackled a similar problem to one that might arise in your own data. For instance, if you are planning on working on an Australian language, it helps to know from the outset that nouns in many of these languages inflect according to an ergative-absolutive pattern, while pronouns are more likely to inflect according to a nominative-accusative pattern. If your chosen language comes from the Oceanic subgroup of the Austronesian family, your preparatory reading will indicate that you can expect to encounter a particularly complex possessive system on nouns. It will not be possible to say exactly how the system will work in any individual language, but you can expect to find some kind of overt grammatical distinction between what we refer to as alienable possession, i.e. the possession of things over which we have some kind of choice, and inalienable possession, which refers to the possession of things where no choice is involved (such as body parts and kin terms).

Choosing a particular language within a larger grouping can be subject to fairly random factors, which often depend on issues of personal preference. For instance, when I first thought about doing fieldwork in Vanuatu as a graduate student, I initially had no particular language in mind. At the time, there was a large number of almost completely undescribed languages, and because there were few researchers active in the area at the time, there was relatively little risk of me stepping on other people's toes. The field was therefore fairly wide open.

I had a personal preference for a language with some morphosyntactic complexity. That meant that while I could avoid the small number of morphologically fairly simple Polynesian languages that are spoken in the country, there were still many dozens of other relatively complex languages left to choose from. I decided that if I were going to do a good job, it would probably be best if I were to choose a location where I stood a reasonable chance of acquiring some kind of a speaking ability in the language. I thought that if I were to work on a large island with many languages, Bislama—the national lingua franca—would possibly become too much of a ready-made crutch, so I decided to restrict my search to small islands where there was just a single language. This reduced the number of choices quite substantially. Of the various options that this left me with, I ended up choosing the Paamese language.

Other budding field linguists have come to me over the years for advice about what language they might work on in the same country. People have all sorts of reasons for wanting to go to particular kinds of places. People who are planning on doing fieldwork with young children in tow have expressed a need for a location which is not too far from a hospital. Others have wanted to be close to an airstrip or an anchorage for ease of access, and from where it would be easy to get out if there was an urgent medical need. Some have wanted to go to a location where there might be other Europeans nearby in case they needed advice about things from their own cultural perspective. Yet others have wanted to go somewhere *without* any other Europeans, presumably to avoid the distraction of familiarity. Some people feel the need to be near a telephone, or near roads, or near a regular supply of electricity so they can charge batteries on equipment that they may have. If you know that you cannot cope without a regular supply of chocolate biscuits, or you have some other special needs that can only be satisfied in a reasonably well-equipped store, you will need to make sure that you choose a field site that has relatively easy access to a store. Of course, some personal preferences are a bit harder to fulfil than others. I know of one budding field linguist, for example, who wanted to go to a tropical field location where there were no spiders!

While individuals vary enormously in the kinds of situations that they can be expected to adapt to, single males may be in a better position in many cases to go to relatively remote locations, while people in families or single females might find it easier to work somewhere a little less remote. But, there can be no hard and fast rules here. I know of single females who have found things perfectly satisfactory in very remote locations, while I know of single males who have struggled to cope with life in places far less remote. Personality obviously plays a major role in how well you will be suited to what kind of field site.

From the outset, you should be prepared to accept that you may not necessarily be the person you think you are, and that you may have a fair amount of learning to do wherever you end up. I would also offer the general advice that once you have made up your mind about where you want to go, you should make sure that you are fully committed to going to that place. Being only half-heartedly committed to a field site is not a good way to start. There are enough things that can make fieldwork more difficult than you originally anticipated so you need to start from a reasonable level of enthusiasm.

3.3 Background work

Let us imagine that you have now settled upon the language that you want to work on. In addition to your general background reading, you will now need to do as much reading as possible on that particular language, or its immediate neighbours, as well as any additional reading on the history of the area, and of the culture of the people. For purely practical matters, it is worth getting hold of a copy of the relevant local travel guidebook. These often include remarkably useful details about transport and accommodation possibilities, as well as pointing out some of the pitfalls to avoid in local travel.

3.3.1 Reading the literature

It may be that little—or even nothing—has ever been written on the language and its neighbours, but often there will be at least *something*. When you read these materials, you will need to be aware that they may not be totally reliable. Any linguistic sources written before the 1940s or 1950s in many parts of the world are likely to have been written by people without any formal training in linguistics, which may mean that phonemic contrasts have been missed, and particular grammatical patterns may have been misrepresented. Even sources written more recently than this can be suspect if the author is an interested amateur rather than a trained linguist. At the same time, there are plenty of examples of early sources written by amateurs which have turned out to represent excellent sources of linguistic data, and you may be lucky enough to be faced with inspired early sources.

If there are any older published materials written in the language in question, you may also want to scour these for useful background information. For many small languages in parts of the world where people's earliest contact with the outside world came with Christian missionaries, you may be able to find some old translations of parts of the Bible, or other kinds of religious literature. I would offer a word of caution about relying too heavily on such materials, particularly in the initial stages of your fieldwork. In my experience, many such translations exhibit grammatical and stylistic oddities that do not correspond closely to normal spoken usage. While local people may have in the meantime come to regard these oddities as indicative of high ecclesiastical style, they often began simply as misanalysed grammatical constructions. If you want to find out how people speak in ordinary day-to-day situations, it would probably not be wise for you to arrive with a knowledge of constructions that remind people more of something like the King James version of their language.

If these kinds of sources date from the nineteenth century or earlier, or even from the early twentieth century, there is every likelihood that those writing the language may have had limited understanding of phonetics. It must also be remembered that in those times, the concept of the phoneme had not been clearly or widely enunciated, so even where a writer shows evidence of good phonetic insight, the resulting written forms may well be phonemically underdifferentiated or overdifferentiated. For example, in the Erromangan language of Vanuatu, missionaries wrote and translated materials into the language between the 1860s and the 1920s. Although there is a phonemic contrast in this language between /k/ and /ɣ/, the velar fricative was either written as k, or it was simply left out.

Even published sources compiled by trained linguists sometimes need to be treated with caution. You can probably assume that an extensive grammar or dictionary has been based on a substantial amount of contact with speakers of the language and that it is more likely to be reliable because of this. A good grammar should say something about the nature and duration of the fieldwork, and the extent of the recorded textual corpus, so it is worth checking to see if the author offers any words along these lines which you can take as reassuring. I know full well that some of the 'conclusions' that I have reached early in my fieldwork have turned out to be wrong, and I am immensely grateful that I did not immediately rush into print. Some linguists, however, have not always been quite that fortunate, or wise.

The shorter the sketch of a language, the greater the possibility that certain facts have been either oversimplified or even incorrectly analysed. Despite what I have just said, I have in the past published short sketches of languages and I have since discovered that some of what I reported is mistaken. For example, I published a twelve-page sketch of the Neve'ei language of Vanuatu (Crowley 2002) which was based exclusively on elicited data from a single speaker. In that sketch, I wrote that the language had only singular and plural pronouns. It turned out, in fact, that there is a separate series of dual pronouns which I had missed because these forms only appear in pragmatically fairly restricted sorts of contexts. I am now faced with the need in any subsequent publications relating to this language to point out my initial error.

Of course, when the only published source for a language is a short wordlist which contains little or no grammatical information, there are all sorts of possibilities for forms to sneak past the compiler incorrectly glossed, phonemically underdifferentiated or overdifferentiated, or grammatically misanalysed. I know of one such wordlist in which the word *labim* appears as a grammatically complex item, consisting of the root *labi-* 'excrement' followed by the possessive suffix *-m* 'your'. It turned out, in fact, that the word *labim* cannot be further analysed grammatically, and that it means 'area where people go to defecate' rather than 'your excrement'.

Further reading: Austin and Crowley (1995).

3.3.2 The linguist and the lingua franca

Part of your pre-departure preparation may require some language learning on your part. There are many parts of the world where people in rural areas speak little or no English. Some other intermediary language may be needed in order for you to be able to speak comfortably with local people, and this will almost certainly be the language in which you conduct your initial elicitation, and possibly even all of your elicitation. Since you are going to be making some fairly fine judgements in this language, your command of it will need to be fairly confident.

If you are keen to go to an area where English is not the main local lingua franca, you will need to put substantial effort into learning that language. In some cases, there may be few opportunities to learn this language before you go into the field. While it will generally be possible to find ways of learning major world languages such as French or Spanish, acquiring a knowledge of Swahili prior to going on fieldwork in East Africa may be more difficult. In some cases, then, you may have to defer this part of your preparation until you arrive in the country itself.

When I first made my decision to do fieldwork in Vanuatu, I knew that I would be operating largely through the medium of Bislama, which is the name by which Melanesian Pidgin is known locally. One linguist had produced a set of language lessons with accompanying tapes for Tok Pisin, the variety of the same language that is spoken in nearby Papua New Guinea, so I began working through those. When I first arrived in Vanuatu, I planned to spend a month learning how to 'convert' my knowledge of Tok Pisin into Bislama. When I finally left for my field site of Paama, while I was certainly not confident in Bislama, I felt that I at least had sufficient command of the language to explain the purpose of my visit.

You have to be prepared for the possibility that things might not be quite as easy as you think. I also decided that since I was going to Vanuatu, it might be a good idea to try to resuscitate my knowledge of high-school French by spending four days in New Caledonia on the way. As a country lad who still liked my meat well done at the time, if not lightly burnt, I discovered the hard way that my progress in French had been much slower than I would have liked. I ordered *steak tartare* in a restaurant and was utterly confident that the English translation of *raw steak* on the back of the menu could not possibly be right. I, however, was wrong, and they were right: it was clearly going to take more than four days to beef up my French. And even though I had put such a lot of effort into my Bislama, something like twenty years later I was reminiscing with somebody about my early days on Paama. He commented that people at the time found it quite difficult to talk to me because I 'couldn't speak Bislama'. At the time, I thought I *was* speaking Bislama, but local people clearly had a somewhat different perception!

3.4 Planning your fieldtrip

If you are embarking on your first fieldtrip, this is likely to be one of the greatest adventures of your life so far. But you are going to have to approach this in a very different way from how you might go about planning for a three-month backpacking holiday in Europe. When you are going on holiday, you don't have to have an itinerary and you can decide on a daily basis what cathedral you are going to visit, whether to go swimming or hiking, or whether to try out some new restaurants. You have no overall goal other than to have a great time.

A fieldtrip is fundamentally different in that you have a very different goal at the end: the documentation of a language. If you are a graduate student, the dissertation that you produce will probably be about 100,000 words long and it will be the most substantial piece of work you have produced so far. If you go on in academia, you may eventually conclude that writing your dissertation was the most demanding thing you ever did. The consequences of failure may be quite severe if your chosen career path depends crucially on successfully completing the dissertation and this will always be lurking in the back of your mind.

What this means is that your fieldtrip needs to be planned. Of course, you should not expect to be able to plan things down to the minutest detail, as one of the things that you will hopefully learn out of your fieldwork experiences is to go with the flow and to adapt to changing circumstances. However, you should have some kind of overall plan in mind. What I want to do now is point to some of the major issues that you will need to think through before you leave for the field.

3.4.1 Fieldwork duration

Perhaps the first decision you will need to make is how long you are going to need in the field. Of course, there is no single answer to a question such as this, as linguistic projects can vary enormously in terms of their goals. However, if your intention is to write a dissertation-length grammar of a language, you should probably aim for a total of between nine and twelve months in the field. You should probably also aim for this period to be spread between two distinct periods of fieldwork with an intermediate period of analysis and preliminary write-up at home.

I would recommend that your first visit be a longer one and that your second visit be somewhat shorter. If you are planning on twelve months in the field, this means that your first visit may be of nine months' duration while your second visit would be of three months. The point of returning home after a substantial initial period in the field is so that you can properly organize your data and so that you can come up with a provisional analysis of what you have already done. It is likely that during this writing up, you will become aware of certain gaps in your data which you were not aware of when you were in the field. This is because you will be in a position to bounce ideas off your colleagues, or your supervisor, and you will have access to a library. You will also have more time to sit and think without interruption. All of this would be difficult—or impossible—if you had stayed in the field. Then, when you return to the field for your final period of data-gathering, you can concentrate on checking the accuracy of material about which you may have developed some doubts during your preliminary write-up, and you can fill the gaps that you have noted.

Having an initial trip with a follow-up trip should be considered essential planning. I have examined one doctoral dissertation which was based on only a single period of fieldwork and the final work that was submitted was replete with statements such as 'Further work is needed to investigate this phenomenon' or 'It is not possible to decide between these two solutions without access to further data.' Such words are anathema to Ph.D. examiners, as well as to pre-publication reviewers of book manuscripts.

Exactly how you should break up your period in the field is going to depend to some extent on your personal circumstances. If you have personal commitments that allow for only an initial fieldtrip of six months, then by all means plan for two equal visits of six months each. You should also be prepared to make changes in your plans as your fieldwork progresses. My original plans for fieldwork on Paama in Vanuatu were for an initial nine-month fieldtrip with a shorter three-month follow-up trip for checking and filling gaps. However, while I had done fieldwork before in Australia, my fieldtrips were always much shorter and more frequent, and I also had access to private spaces where I could work comfortably with electric lighting. On Paama, I had no table. (People eat on mats on the floor.) There was also no electricity. (People use kerosene lamps and torches at night.) There was also little opportunity for privacy. (People would typically want to come and chat if they saw me working by myself.)

While I was accumulating lots of textual data and I had done a lot of direct elicitation, I started to feel that I was floundering after about six months and I had little idea of the directions in which further elicitation should go. My lexical data was a mess because I had no opportunity to organize things properly. I therefore made the decision to jump on a ship back to the capital and then to return to Australia to do some serious writing up. I remember that my return three months early annoyed the head of my department at the time, but I placated him with a promise to spend six months on my second fieldtrip instead of the three months that was originally planned. That's what I did, and when I went back with properly organized lexical material and some clearly set-out provisional analysis, I was back in the swing of things for much more productive elicitation. My second trip ended up being so much more worthwhile and so much more enjoyable than the first.

3.4.2 Planning for contingencies

You are going to have to plan for a variety of contingencies in the field. Some level of self-sufficiency may be necessary in health matters, depending on where you are going. Malaria is an unpleasant disease which can certainly leave you debilitated for a few weeks, and it can sometimes be worse than simply debilitating. However, it is largely preventable. You need to visit your doctor before you leave for a prescription for malarial prophylaxis. What you will find is that there is a range of options and you should discuss these with your doctor. Some treatments have nasty side effects with small numbers of people. It would be a good idea to establish which medication is most suitable for you, as it would not be a good idea if you were to take a medication-induced psychotic turn in the field. This happened to me once, so I threw the tablets down the toilet . . . and then came down with malaria as a result.

Obviously, malaria is not the only potential health problem. Depending on where you are going, vaccinations for a number of different communicable diseases may be required, or at least recommended. You should therefore inform your doctor where you are going and talk things over with him or her well before you leave. There are parts of the world where HIV/AIDS is a major public health issue, so a high level of personal responsibility can also reduce the risk of coming down with health problems.

Even minor health problems need to be catered for when you are in the field. I never leave for the field without a supply of antibiotic powder or cream, bandaids, and antifungal medication. A simple scratch or a mosquito bite can easily become infected in the tropics and this can ultimately develop into a serious ulcer. Be sure to take more medication than you think you might possibly need for yourself, as you will quite possibly end up tending to local people's minor cuts and scrapes as well.

If you are the sort of person who happens to come down with whatever minor ailment is going around whenever you get run down, then perhaps it would also be a good idea to pack a supply of nutritional supplements. I also find that if I am doing a lot of walking or other kind of physical activity, small sachets of rehydration salts can be a life-saver.

Further reading: Samarin (1967: 71–4).

3.5 Funding

Linguistic fieldwork is seldom cheap, and unless you are a person of independent means, you will almost certainly need some kind of funding support to back you up in your endeavours. If you already have an academic position, your salary costs will be taken care of, but if you are a graduate student, you will need some kind of stipend, and possibly also support for the payment of your fees. Obviously, opportunities will vary from country to country, though sometimes funding agencies do allow for grant applications to cover costs such as these.

Fieldwork is also going to involve direct travel-related costs. This will include your fares to and from your field site, which may involve an expensive international ticket as well as additional fares from the capital to the local community where you are going to be working. Travel insurance is crucial, because you never know what might go wrong medically to require you to return to the capital, or perhaps even to your home country for treatment. You are going to need reliable recording equipment. You are also likely to be faced with fees for the issuing of visas and research permits. You will need to have some money to cover your living expenses in your host community, as store-bought goods in remote locations can sometimes be fearsomely expensive. Finally, you will need to have funds with which you can pay your 'informants'.

It is obviously impossible to say precisely what kind of amounts you should budget for, as this is going to depend on the specific situation. I know of some linguists who have done all of their linguistic research while staying in a hotel or a local guesthouse, while others have had no option but to stay within the community in local-style housing. Obviously there can be a substantial difference in costs involved. Of course, those who choose to stay in a hotel when there is a possibility of local accommodation within the community are likely to miss important opportunities for observing natural linguistic interaction, and this is a factor to be considered alongside that of cost.

Once you have worked out your budget, you will need to seek funding. You may be lucky enough to be attached to a university where there are internal mechanisms for funding this kind of research. Increasingly, though, funding these days needs to come from external agencies. There are some bodies which call for applications specifically to support research leading to basic linguistic documentation of the kind that I am talking about in this volume, including the following:

- The Hans Rausing Endangered Languages Project (www.eldp. soas.ac.uk/hrelp_home.htm);
- The Foundation for Endangered Languages (www.ogmios.org/ home.htm);
- The Endangerd Languages Fund (www.ling.yale.edu/~elf);
- The Volkswagenstiftung (www.volkswagen-stiftung.de).

None of these funding agencies is in a position to fund all projects that are submitted, so they typically look for evidence that a project is well thought out logistically, that it has community support, that it shows promise of producing results that will directly benefit the local community in some way, and, of course, that it is of substantial academic merit.

In addition to these funds which are specifically geared towards supporting linguistic research, there are other funding agencies which call for academically sound applications from a broad range of disciplines conducted by scholars in your country. Since you may be competing with other projects to investigate evolving attitudes to mental illness in sixteenth-century France, the deconstruction of the writings of postmodern writers in Brunei, and the genetic modification of newts in Britain, it is much more difficult to give specific advice on how to 'sell' a project involving linguistic documentation. However, such funds typically stress academic excellence and the proven research record of the participating researchers, so it is important to pay close attention to these kinds of issues.

3.6 Permits

Depending on where it is that you intend to carry out your fieldwork, there will be a range of bureaucratic procedures that you will probably have to deal with. Even if there should happen to be no bureaucratic requirements relating to access to a particular fieldwork project, there is an overriding ethical requirement that the general aims of the project should be understood by the community you will be working with, as well as accepted by people in that community. A linguist should therefore not just turn up on the beach or at the airstrip and expect immediately to move into data-gathering mode.

Quite apart from normal passport and visa requirements, there may well be a specific procedure to follow in some countries if a researcher is planning to conduct linguistic research. A researcher may need to be issued with a special research visa, which has conditions—and possibly also fees—attached to it, which distinguish it from an ordinary tourist visa. While a tourist visa will often be granted automatically for a short stay on arrival at an international airport, a research visit may require a longer stay, and immigration officers may not be authorized to issue those sorts of permits on arrival at the airport.

You also need to be aware that your proposed site may turn out to be one where national authorities do not welcome the prying eyes of outsiders, in which case you may never be granted a visa. I understand that it is very difficult for outsiders to gain permission from Indian authorities to visit parts of the Andaman Islands, so unless you have very good local contacts and very good reasons for wanting to go there, it is perhaps not worth trying. I had originally intended carrying out my own doctoral research on a particular island in Indonesia in 1976, but my application for a permit was met with prolonged silence from the Indonesian end to the point where I was losing valuable scholarship time. I then made my own decision to switch to Paama in Vanuatu as an alternative field site. This was just as well, really, as it turned out that the island in Indonesia that I had chosen to go to, unbeknown to me, hosted a facility in which political prisoners at the time were rumoured to be detained. That meant that I was possibly never going to get that visa anyway.

Even if you are planning on doing research in your own country where the question of visas does not arise, it is likely that you will need to seek some kind of formal approval from the local community where you are planning on conducting research. The nature of such local authorities, as well as their powers, will no doubt vary from place to place, but it will be your job to find out what the proper procedures are, and to follow those procedures. Simply arriving on the doorstep will probably not ensure a warm welcome if a local community has already given considerable thought to establishing a set of procedures to deal with the involvement of people such as yourself within the community.

Research permits may need to be sorted out before arrival in the country concerned, either through the country's diplomatic mission in your own country, or directly through the relevant agencies in the country itself. Researchers who simply arrive in a country expecting to be granted permission to carry out fieldwork may sometimes find that they are required to leave the country again and apply for permission from outside. There will normally be some local agency which has the primary responsibility for initiating the issue of a research permit. This may be the relevant National Museum, the Department of Immigration, or the Department of Culture. It is always best to have some kind of local contact in order that you know the correct place to address your application, as well as the appropriate format. If you are unable to work out the appropriate procedure, you may be able to get valuable help from linguists in a local university. Fortunately, in this era of internet searches, finding appropriate contacts is much easier than it once was.

Granting of permission to conduct research may be associated with the payment of some kind of fee to the local institution. Local institutions involved in culture and language are often not well supplied with funds from their national governments, so this kind of contribution from visiting foreign researchers helps in a small way in the running of the museum. It also makes perfect sense for national museums to coordinate research in this way, in part to ensure that there is complementarity between researchers. It would not be wise for several linguists to descend on a single language community when there may be other languages nearby that have been completely neglected. Channelling research in this way also ensures that there is not a sudden influx into a single community at the same time of a linguist, an anthropologist, a botanist, and a seismologist. In order to reduce any possible negative impact of foreign visitors, research should again be distributed as widely as possible.

Sometimes, the procedures for gaining permission to carry out research in a community may be unclear, and the fieldworker can easily be caught in the middle of competing powers. In the 1960s in Queensland, the European 'manager' of an Aboriginal reserve had absolute power to decide who could enter and stay on the reserve and who could not, and he (it was never a she, as far as I know) did not have to consult with members of the local community. By the early 1970s, local Aboriginal communities were beginning to establish their own procedures for who could enter reserves, but there was something of a power struggle between the old managers and the new community councils.

When I first arrived in far north Queensland to carry out my research on the Uradhi and Mpakwithi languages, I had made arrangements with the chairperson of the local community council, who was agreeable to my research project. I duly arrived to start my research and just after breakfast on my first morning there, I received a message requiring me to appear immediately at the manager's office. I realized that I had been caught up in a nasty mess and I was trembling by the time I arrived at the manager's office. I somehow managed to convince him that since I had the approval of the community council, I should be allowed to stay, but it was quite clear to me that he was not happy about this. I am convinced that he would have put me on the first plane out of there if he could have managed it.

In some parts of the world, the granting of official permits, the payment of bribes, and arbitrary vindictiveness seem to go more or less hand in hand. Fortunately, my own rather more positive experiences leave me completely unqualified to offer any specific advice to any fieldworker who faces these kinds of administrative norms. As advance warning for some, and as entertainment for others, I simply recommend that you read Barley's (1983) *The Innocent Anthropologist: Notes from a Mud Hut.*

3.7 Equipment and supplies

While most of my fieldwork recordings were on reel-to-reel or cassette tape, new recording technologies allow you to record high-quality digital audio and video and then work with it directly on your computer.

3.7.1 Recording gear

Basically, the only equipment that an ordinary project will need in the field is a reliable recorder and high-quality microphone, as well as an ample supply of batteries. Some projects are more sophisticated than this, calling for video recording of interpersonal communication or public speeches to capture visual aspects of communication in conjunction with ordinary grammatical patterns. And having now tried the luxury of a laptop in the field, I can see why many other linguists might want to do the same.

If you are going to rely on batteries, you will need to make sure that you have a good supply of the best-quality batteries. If batteries are available locally in the field, I have found that they are often the cheaper batteries which drain more quickly, because local people are not able to afford the more expensive long-life batteries. In any case, if you need a special size of battery, you may not be able to get what you need at all. This means that you may need to estimate your battery needs for several months and bring them with you. Of course, batteries are heavy and you may find yourself paying quite a surcharge if you have to pay excess baggage to bring them with you on the plane.

The more equipment you have, the more likely it is that you will need regular access to electricity. You may be lucky enough to be working in an area where there is 24-hour electricity. Of course, electricity supplies in some parts of the world operate on 110 volts while other parts of the world operate on 220 (or 240) volts. If your equipment is not compatible with both, you may need to carry a voltage adaptor. Different countries also operate with different kinds of plugs and if you do not have a proper converter, then your equipment may end up being totally useless in the field where adaptors may well not be available locally.

In some field sites, if you are going to be dependent on an electricity supply, you may need to acquire your own generator. The average city-dwelling linguist has probably not had much contact with generators, but even the most portable of portable generators is not really very portable. They are, in fact, quite bulky and heavy enough that it takes at least two people to carry one. So, with all of this equipment, you might even need a vehicle (or a boat) to transport it all. These days, adventurers and travellers are increasingly making use of portable solar panels to charge the batteries of their equipment, and field linguists can make use of this kind of technology as well.

The price of all of this equipment is starting to mount well beyond what will be available for the average graduate student. It also means that a simple trek across the island with your recording equipment in your backpack may well be out of the question given the amount of additional gear that you would have to bring with you to keep everything operating. What is most practical and what is ideal often do not go hand in hand in field research.

Let's go back to the audio recorder. Until fairly recently, any advice would have revolved around what sort of cassette, recorder and cassette tape to use. Many people still record on cassettes, though the information that they contain is increasingly being digitized when it is deposited for storage in professionally curated linguistic archives. Cassette recorders are fast becoming obsolete and digital technology has advanced to the point where it is preferable to record material digitally in the first place.

There are several ways of recording digitally, but the preferred option at the moment is to record with flashram recorders.

Some linguists also record on minidisc recorders. While the quality of sound reproduction of minidiscs is fine for transcribing and listening to texts, the proprietary playback mechanism, as well as the process of transfer from minidisc to your computer, results in the loss of significant parts of the sound signal. This renders the material less useful for anybody who might want to conduct instrumental analysis of your data in the future. There are also questions about the archivability of the proprietary formats used by minidiscs, so they need to be converted to wav files as soon as practicable. Best fieldwork practice at the moment is to record with flashram recorders in preference to minidiscs.

If you are going to be transcribing from a cassette recorder, you will need to make sure that the equipment you have brought with you allows for easy and rapid rewind, and that you are able to rewind short stretches of text at a time. It can be very frustrating for both you and your language-helper if you hit the rewind button and it takes so long for the mechanism to react that you end up hearing all over again material that you have already dealt with. The machine also needs to be quite sturdy, as you are likely to be hitting that rewind button thousands of times while you are in the field. A digital recorder will come equipped with some kind of digital equivalent of a rewind button. It would be a good idea to practise using this before you go to the field so that you can work out how to reverse to the place that you want to get to.

Your audio recorder may need to be small enough that you can carry it in your pack over sometimes rough terrain. It will need to be sturdy. I have on one occasion had to dive into the ocean to rescue a tape recorder after the outriggers on the canoe broke and the tape recorder and I went into the drink together. (Fortunately, the tape recorder was in a waterproof bag, and I was able to rescue it after only a few seconds on the bottom before the salt water got to it.) You can also expect to get rained on from time to time, and tropical rain tends not to be the gentle drizzle of many temperate western cities. Then, there is the possibility of cyclones—also known as typhoons or hurricanes, depending where you live—which can cause considerable water damage to equipment, especially in thatch houses that are built to allow for a cooling through-flow of air in a tropical climate.

While many recorders come with an in-built microphone, you should not use it as it will also record machine noise, and it is typically not of sufficient quality for fieldwork recording. You will get far better quality recordings if you use a plug-in external microphone. Microphones come in all sorts of shapes, sizes, and capabilities, depending on what sort of recording you are going to be doing, and you can find good advice on websites linked from your favourite linguistic archive.

One option would be a clip-on lapel microphone, which has the advantage of being very discreet. However, this would be useful if only one person were speaking. Even when I am recording monologues, I always like to introduce my speaker, as well as giving the date and place in which the recording takes place, and it would be an awkward way to start a recording session if I were to get things rolling by speaking into somebody else's sternum. A flat microphone that sits directly on the table can be fairly discreet, while also picking up voices in more than one direction, though this kind of microphone has a nasty habit of picking up all sorts of noises of people fidgeting and tapping on the table unless you remember to lay it down on a piece of folded cloth. Finally, there is the traditional hand-held microphone, which has the disadvantage of making the fieldworker look like a journalist in a disaster scene, though you can hold the microphone in the ideal position for the best-quality recording, or put it in a stand that will soon be ignored by the speaker.

Further reading: Austin (2006).

3.7.2 Other needs

You will require a supply of stationery. This means that you will have to anticipate how much notepaper you will need, as well as how many pens you are likely to use. You will also need to anticipate expectations from the community that your ample supply of paper and pens may be publicly fairly available to allow people to write letters, as it may often be difficult for people to get hold of such items. Remember, though, that while stationery is not expensive to buy, it can be heavy, and if you have to transport it by air to your field site, you can easily use up most of your free airline baggage allowance, leaving you facing a bill for excess baggage that you had not budgeted for.

You need to remember that you may not always have a table to work on. A clipboard is therefore a very useful item to bring with you to ensure that you have a solid surface to write on. I would recommend that you buy bound notebooks rather than loose-leaf binders or writing tablets with tear-out pages. I have tried both of these options in the field in the past and neither was very satisfactory. With loose-leaf binders, the holes on the pages often tear through and your pages then become free-floating entities which can either end up in the wrong place, or they can get lost altogether. The same applies to tear-out pages from writing tablets. Such pages are good for writing letters or for scribbled notes, but they are not good for any information which you want to keep as part of a permanent record.

A field researcher needs to anticipate any possible special food needs. Local food may be nutritious but bland, or it may be overly spicy, and sometimes unfamiliar tastes and textures may be difficult for the newly arrived fieldworker to cope with at first. Depending on the personal circumstances of the researcher, it may or may not be easy to prepare your own food in your field site. If you cannot prepare your own food and you have an urge for familiar tastes, textures, and species, it is best to bring some items with you. Some of your favourite items may be expensive, and they may have to be shared communally. (However, I have on occasion been known to hide tins of baked beans in my suitcase and eat them when nobody else is around.) When the food is bland, your personal supply of chili sauce, soy sauce, or tomato sauce may help.

Taking care of personal preferences can extend beyond your dietary requirements. For example, if you have a resistance to the idea of using coconut husks or leaves for sanitary purposes, you will need to bring in an adequate supply of toilet paper, and you may need to protect it fiercely. (I have in the past kept mine hidden under my bed until the precise moment of intended use.) In a field site where there is no electricity, you will need your own torch (or flashlight), as well as a kerosene lamp. And a kerosene lamp is not much use without matches.

If you know you are going to have to do some trekking, be sure to invest in some properly fitting hiking boots. One pair of boots that I took into the field allowed too much forward movement of my foot on downhill sections. When I arrived at my destination and took my socks off, one of my big toenails more or less came off with the sock, and the other one came off by itself a few days later. A comfortable pack is also a good investment. If you are heading for somewhere tropical, a waterproof pack is a wise investment. Even if you don't get caught in a tropical downpour, you would be surprised how much sweat can run off your back, into the contents of your pack, and right through all of your once fresh-smelling clothes.

Apart from your major equipment items, given what I have said so far in this chapter, you should therefore consider including the following items on your shopping list in preparation for leaving for your field location:

- good hiking boots and pack
- kerosene lamp and torch (or flashlight)
- special food treats
- clipboard
- pens
- one or two pocket-sized notebooks
- good supply of hard-cover bound notebooks
- batteries for torch and recording equipment
- tapes for recording
- regular prescription medication
- dietary supplements, rehydration salts
- injections and prophylactic medication
- antibiotic and antifungal medication, bandaids

3.8 Getting about in the field

The kinds of locations where field research takes place are typically fairly remote. Arrival may be by small plane, coastal vessel, speedboat, canoe, or on the back of a truck. Any trip that is more than a short one is likely to involve a degree of discomfort, and some walking may be necessary to reach your final destination. For instance, when I was doing fieldwork on Erromango, I faced a forty-five-minute flight from the capital. I was then faced with the possibility of a fairly expensive three-hour speedboat trip if the sea was sufficiently calm. If the sea was rough, or if the local boat-owner ran out of fuel (which often happened), then I was faced with a 22-kilometre walk. The first 11 kilometres followed a logging track, though with the suspension of logging, this had started to revert to bush. The initial stage in the process of regeneration to bush involved a dense growth of *Mimosa pudica*, a treacherous grass with razor sharp backwards-pointing thorns that leave your legs from ankle to thigh looking like you've just spent a bad night on a bed of nails. (The local name for *Mimosa pudica* is *gras nil* 'nail grass'.)

After that, the vehicular road gave out completely and the remaining 11 kilometres involved a single-file bush track that crossed a dozen or so streams, including two major rivers, all without bridges. There was some steep—and often slippery—climbing, and all of this is done while carrying a pack. A field linguist has to be either fit before arrival, or he or she very rapidly becomes fit in this kind of situation. Failure to cope with these conditions can be unpleasant. I heard of one American Peace Corps volunteer on Erromango who simply gave up in the middle of a trek. He collapsed in tears on the path and in the end he had to be returned stateside. In fact, I remember once in a state of exhaustion starting to think very seriously about doing the same myself. I just wanted to curl up beneath an overhanging rock and sleep on the ground to see if I had the strength—or the will-power—to continue the next morning.

There may be other travel options. If you are going to be based on a river or by the sea, it pays to learn how to row a canoe if that is one of the local means of transport. This can be not only convenient, but also relaxing for short journeys. Of course, you may lack advanced rowing skills and the consequences can be dire. I have already mentioned my misfortune in a canoe when an outrigger snapped off, causing the canoe to capsize. What I failed to mention at that point was that the accident was my fault: I had failed to align the canoe properly according to the direction of the swell in a turbulent part of the sea.

The potential unreliability of transport has to be taken as a major factor in planning one's fieldwork. For instance, if your only access in and out of a particular location is by scheduled twice-weekly flights or by a weekly ship, you cannot always assume that the plane or ship will arrive as scheduled. Anything at all could happen to leave you stranded for longer than you had hoped. It might rain heavily and the grass airstrip might take a couple of days to dry. The grass on the airstrip might not have been cut by the local community so the pilot cannot land. The passage of a cyclone can close down an entire air or sea transportation grid for days. The plane or ship might break down with no replacement possible. The plane or ship might be diverted at the last minute to deal with a medical emergency somewhere else. A local politician might use his or her influence to divert a plane or ship from its proper schedule to pick him or her up. A fieldworker should, therefore, never rely on tight travel connections, especially if you are dealing with your international flight out of the country. Always allow sufficient spare time in transit.

Of course, being delayed does not have to be an unmitigated disaster. On a short non-fieldwork-related visit to the island of Malakula in 1988, just as I was ready to fly back to the capital to return to work, the heavens opened up and the airstrip turned to a mudpit. A local man suddenly saw an advantage in my distress. He took me by the hand and said, 'I am one of the last speakers of the Nāti language. Now that you are stuck here, we will go to the local store and get some pens and some exercise books and we will spend the time documenting my language.' And that is what we did for several days till the sun dried off the airstrip and the planes started flying again (Crowley 1998*a*).

3.9 First contact

Your arrival in your chosen field site is likely to be the scariest part of your entire fieldwork. There are some things you can do to make this easier.

3.9.1 Arriving with an invitation

When I was talking earlier about choosing a language, I did not say that the best way of all to choose a language is for the language community to choose you. The luckiest field linguist is somebody who is invited into a community (e.g. Hale 2001). Sometimes, the project design may be predetermined by the community, in which case it is up to the linguist to decide whether he or she can match the community's expectations with his or her own. In other cases, a community may arrange for a linguist to come in and do certain things that the community wants done, with the *quid pro quo* that the linguist will be allowed to write a grammar for his or her doctorate.

Such invitations to participate in community-run projects can arise in a variety of ways. In many parts of Australia, for example, there are community-run 'language centres' which have been set up as archives for linguistic data and for the storage of oral tradition and cultural knowledge. Language centres like these often publicly advertise for linguists to come and service their needs. In other cases, a community may be keen to develop literacy materials for young children in conjunction with moves at the national level towards greater use of local languages in the formal education system and they may seek the help of a linguist. A community may also be keen to see the Bible or some other important religious document translated into their language. The Summer Institute of Linguistics (www.sil.org) has an international network of trained linguists who respond to such community requests in many different parts of the world.

Even if you do not have a formal invitation to come to work in a community, it is always best to be introduced into the community either by somebody who is a member of the community, or by somebody who is at least well known to local people. My work on the Erromangan language began more or less by accident. I accepted an invitation from an Erromangan friend to come and spend Christmas with him and his family in his village in 1993. It was such a wonderful place, and people were so overwhelmingly welcoming, that my friend suggested that since I was a linguist, wouldn't it be a good idea to come and spend more time in his village so I could document his language. This hadn't entered my mind during that initial visit, but being invited into the community in this way seemed like an opportunity that was too good to miss. So, I floated this idea past other people in the community. They responded enthusiastically, and I subsequently spent just over a year living on that island, and produced both a grammar and a dictionary of the language, as well as a collection of oral tradition.

3.9.2 Arriving without an invitation

Many intending field linguists don't have the advantage that I had on Erromango of already knowing people who can introduce you into a community. This is most likely to be the case with graduate students who may be just starting out on their fieldwork careers. In fact, this was the situation that I faced when I had first made my decision to work on the Paamese language. I shudder when I think back to how I started, but will contrast my arrival on Erromango with my arrival on Paama in order to convince people that this is not the best way to start.

I arrived in the country unannounced, knowing not a single soul. The first thing I did was present myself to the local authorities for the necessary permits. This did not seem to be a major problem, as nobody really seemed to have given much thought to the need for any kind of procedure for dealing with this kind of visitor at the time. I then presented myself to the local museum, where an overseas linguist was in charge. He put me in touch with some Paamese people living in town and I spent a few weeks talking to people on a daily basis to record some basic linguistic information, and also to learn something about the island itself.

At that time, there were no phones on Paama, nor was there an airstrip. This meant that it was not going to be possible to forewarn anybody of my impending visit in time for my planned arrival. The only regular way to get to the island at the time was by ship. The use of that term suggests a grandness that is perhaps a little inappropriate, as the *MV Frances* was really just a largish boat that plied the open Pacific Ocean. The one-day journey to Paama was hugely uncomfortable. The only place to lie down was on a canvas sheet that was stretched out over the cover of the cargo hold. I was seasick. I suffered additional discomfort because I didn't realize that there was a toilet on board, and I was too embarrassed to ask somebody. (In any case, on subsequent trips, it became apparent that holding it in wasn't necessarily the worst option.)

When the vessel finally arrived at Paama and I staggered onto the beach, I do not remember exactly what my first words were to the people who I met, but I suspect it must have been something like 'Take me to your chief'. I do remember that I managed to get myself ensconced in a guesthouse for visitors and then I set off on foot to visit the chiefs of each one of the twenty separate villages on the island to explain the purpose of my visit. Although my visit was completely unexpected, I remember thinking that people were remarkably welcoming. Despite not having arrived under what I would now consider the proper circumstances, I thought that I had probably made a reasonable sort of first impression.

3.9.3 Local reactions to the fieldworker

I also found out about twenty years later that some people thought that when I first arrived on Paama, I was a lunatic. I eventually observed that local people were very tolerant of people with psychological disturbances as long as they were harmless, which was probably just as well. My advice now would be: if it is at all possible, arrange to be introduced to a community by somebody who is known in the community.

Although my arrival on Paama must have seemed rather bizarre to local people, I am sure that those few weeks that I had spent in the capital carrying out some preliminary fieldwork certainly helped convince people that I was not totally mad. There is a lot to be said for getting some kind of introduction to the language before you go to your chosen field site. Sometimes, even being able to say 'hello', 'goodbye', and 'where is the toilet?' as soon as you arrive is going to impress people in the community in a way that will help make people a little more relaxed about your presence.

When I arrived on Paama, I was able to demonstrate that I knew a little of the language already. People were keen to see how far my knowledge went. At one point, a rooster sauntered past and somebody asked me 'Do you know what that's called?' People waited to see if I knew the word *ato* 'chicken'. In fact, all I had recorded at that stage were the words *tōtoman* 'rooster' and *tōletau* 'hen', so I replied with the more specific term. Evidently such a detailed and specific response had been completely unexpected and people quite literally screamed with what I took to be either amazement or delight. I had quite by accident shown myself to be a good language learner, and this no doubt helped to get me started. I may have been mad, but I wasn't totally stupid.

However, the fieldworker must be prepared for the possibility that the project that he or she sees as being thoroughly worthy may not be so positively viewed from within the community itself. In addition to any official permits that may be needed for your research, you will also need to gain community acceptance of your project. In some cases, a local community may reject a project simply because it has misunderstood the intent of the researcher. It is also possible for a project to become a convenient focal point for the expression of local divisions, which can lead to its rejection.

For instance, when I proposed to go to Erromango to conduct research in 1994, my request was initially rejected by the local council of chiefs. The local sponsor of my project was not somebody who I chose, as this aspect of the approval procedure was automatically handled by the National Museum. It turned out that the person who proposed and supported my project on the island was perceived as being sympathetic to a political party that was disfavoured by some of the chiefs at the time. In addition, that person came from a part of the island that had for a long time resisted the granting of permission to Malaysian logging companies to conduct their operations on land belonging to people in his area, whereas some of the chiefs on the council were sympathetic to the granting of logging permits.

Even though I had no idea that this sort of thing was going on, and the chiefs in question had never met me, there was perhaps a suspicion that I might be used as some kind of weapon against Malaysian logging companies. Although my research project had no relevance to either side of the political divide or to the granting of logging permits, it was initially turned down because it provided a convenient way of 'getting at' somebody else on the basis of purely local concerns. It turned out in the end that my own sympathies on this logging issue were very much in line with those on the island who were opposed to the Malaysian logging company. However, despite this sympathy, I was extremely reluctant for a long time to voice any opinion either way on the logging issue because of the potentially divisive nature of this issue, its lack of direct relevance to my linguistic research, and the possibility that some chiefs might call for my expulsion.

In some places, there is resistance to the idea of field research because communities—and sometimes even individuals—feel as if they have already been over-researched. There is a common joke that among a certain group of people, the nuclear family consists of a husband and wife, two children, and a linguist or an anthropologist. If there has been a history of researchers passing through a community in a continuous stream, it is understandable that they may be reluctant to welcome yet another visitor. In some cases, you may simply have to accept that the proposal to which you have given so much thought is not going to go ahead for this kind of reason. You may need to learn to be humble and to find another field site where you *are* welcome. There is little point going somewhere where you are not welcome.

Further reading: Samarin (1967: 10–19).

4

Gathering your Data

One of the most commonly asked questions that non-linguists—and sometimes even linguists of the armchair variety—have asked me about the conduct of fieldwork is: How do you actually start when you are going to describe the phonology, the morphology, and the syntax of a language? That's a perfectly reasonable question, of course, so let's get on with it.

Further reading: Samarin (1967: 45–74), Austin (2006), Bouquiaux and Thomas (1992: 27–38), Vaux and Cooper (1999: 21–2).

4.1 Choosing language-helpers

As soon as you are ready to get started, you are going to need people's help to learn the language. You may arrive with the idea that anybody at all can perform this kind of role, as long as he or she can speak the language in question. Of course, things can be rather more complicated than this. A field guide such as this therefore needs to provide some kind of advice in the selection of an 'informant'.

4.1.1 'Informants'

But before we consider the issue of who is going to help you to work on the language, I want to talk briefly about terminology. In the past, fieldworkers often referred to their 'informants' in the field. While some fieldworkers still use this term, many people feel uncomfortable referring to people in this way. This is because an 'informant' is often taken to be somebody who tells us things that are not meant to become public knowledge, rather like an 'informer'.

The problem is to find another word that clearly indicates the role that our 'informant' plays without expressing this kind of negative connotation. Some people use the term 'consultant', though this has its own negative connotations in many parts of the developing world where self-appointed experts are often contracted on highly paid short-term 'consultancies' to write reports that show little real awareness of the situation on the ground. Some people use the term 'field assistant', or 'language teacher'. Depending on how actively involved in the final materials this person is, it may be legitimate to refer to him or her as also your 'colleague' or your 'collaborator'. In the heading for this section, I have chosen the compound 'language-helper'.

All of these terms may sometimes sound a little forced, or they may not quite match the kind of working relationship that develops. There are therefore times when I try to sidestep these issues of stylistic awkwardness by simply referring to 'the person who I am working with', 'the person who is helping me with my analysis', or even 'somebody who provides native-speaker judgements' if any of these expressions happens to sound better in any given context.

Further reading: Newman and Ratliff (2001: 2–4), Rice (to appear), Bouquiaux and Thomas (1992: 31), Vaux and Cooper (1999: 10).

4.1.2 Language-helpers at home

You may be lucky enough to be in a position to do some work on the language that you are interested in with somebody at home before you even leave for the field. This person may be living in your city for a variety of reasons. He or she may be there as a university student, as a recent immigrant, as a refugee, or as a short-term visitor. One thing that you can probably be certain of is that he or she did not come to your city in order to become somebody's language-helper. An approach from you for help in this kind of matter will almost certainly come as a surprise, and people may not always know quite how to respond.

I remember once approaching a speaker of Nauruan who was living in Canberra when I was still a student there to see if she would be interested in working with me and a small group of other linguists on her language. We were particularly excited by this prospect because Nauruan was a poorly described language which appeared to exhibit a number of unusual features for a member of the Oceanic subgroup of Austronesian languages. I visited this person at her home and explained the situation. She seemed surprised but was willing to participate, so we arranged a time to meet to begin recording sessions. Just as I was leaving and the door closed, I heard very loud shrieks of laughter emanating from inside the house as she told her room-mate what I had come for.

You may well be dealing with a well-educated member of the local community who is in your country to undertake graduate study. If you approach such a person to help you, that person may be reluctant, saying that he or she does not speak the language well enough. This may be based on a realistic assessment of that person's competence, as many people who are well educated enough to get to university overseas have often spent a significant part of their life away from their home communities. If they grew up in town rather than in a rural area, they may not speak their parents' language well at all, or they may speak it with reduced confidence. People who harbour these kinds of feelings may be concerned that they may give you incorrect data. Because such anxiety may be associated with a sense of embarrassment, they may be reluctant to get involved in a research project, and it may be difficult for them to say why because of this sense of embarrassment.

On the other hand, this kind of assessment of someone's linguistic ability may be unrealistic in the sense that he or she may well have a perfectly good command of the kinds of things that you are interested in, such as basic vocabulary, as well as a full command of the phonology, morphology, and syntax. It is only natural that such people may not have a full command of rhetorical styles or arcane vocabulary. However, if you are just starting your work on a previously undescribed language, this does not really matter all that much, as you would need to get this kind of basic information down first before you need to start thinking about the frills. Your initial task, then, will be to reassure your reluctant language-helper that he or she really *can* help you in a meaningful way.

When you start your initial round of elicitation, you should be prepared to meet with a variety of kinds of responses to your requests to record linguistic data from speakers of little-known languages. In general, I have found that such requests meet with an enthusiastic response. People are often keen for their language to be documented, as they may be aware of what has happened to other languages which have suffered from neglect in the past. There are likely to be other positive responses to your expression of interest in describing their language. I once arranged for a speaker of a Vanuatu language to pronounce some words for one of my linguistics courses to give my students some practice in phonetic transcription. Every time he said a word in his language, he giggled. When I asked him what was making him giggle, he said he felt very strange as he had never uttered words in his language to Europeans before. He said it felt 'odd', to the point where he could not suppress the urge to laugh.

However, such positive responses may be tempered with a number of other responses as well. You should not assume that working on somebody's language is automatically going to be a straightforward process once you get started. Initial enthusiasm may gradually—or even quickly—wane when it is discovered that this kind of work usually involves a fairly long-term commitment on the part of the speaker of the language. Initial enthusiasm can easily enough turn to boredom, as you will sometimes find it necessary to complete repetitive morphological paradigms to get the full details of allomorphic variation. Also, the person you are working with may agree to work with you when he or she is not particularly busy, but if that person has other commitments, their workload may well build up to the point where they cannot spare the time to see you as regularly as they could in the past. Missed appointments can be frustrating for you, but they may be unavoidable for the other person.

You also have to be prepared for other kinds of reactions. I know of one linguist who was well known for his ability to acquire a basic speaking ability in any language that he had worked on, and to retain this ability for many years. One story goes that this linguist was somewhere in Queensland and he recognized a stranger in the street as being a likely speaker of a language that he had worked on in the past in Papua New Guinea from his facial features. He addressed this chap in a friendly sort of way in his own language, but his response was to turn tail and run. In all probability, he had entered Australia illegally across the somewhat porous boundary between Papua New Guinea and Queensland, probably by canoe or small boat, and had thought he could pass as a local indigenous person. Anybody who is illegally in your country may be understandably unwilling to act as a language-helper for the unwelcome visibility that this role may provide.

4.1.3 Language-helpers in the field

Carrying out research in the field is likely to proceed in a different way and at a different pace from the way you might proceed when researching the same language 'at home'. Many linguists set out to choose a single individual who is to become their language-helper on a regular basis. Typically this person will be paid at a locally appropriate level for his or her time. With any arrangement that you come to, you need to keep in mind the fact that this person is going to have certain family and communal obligations, which means that you will not always be able to have access to your language-helper whenever you might want. Having arrangements with several people at once is one way of overcoming this problem.

Choosing the right person, or people, to work with can sometimes be quite an issue. If you are going to be working at close quarters with somebody for many months at a stretch, it is not just a question of certain individuals being capable language-helpers and others being incapable. Interpersonal considerations also come into play here, so somebody who is a good language-helper for me may not necessarily be a good language-helper for you, simply because we are two different people.

If you enter into some kind of formal contract-like agreement with a particular person, it can sometimes be difficult—or impossible—to 'dismiss' him or her because this may cause more than just ill will between you and your former language-helper. If that person happens to have been an important member of the community—a chief, perhaps, or a religious leader—then the ill will may come from the entire community. I therefore try to have a much looser arrangement with language-helpers whereby I can call upon somebody's services when I need help, as long as that person is available. This means that I can call upon somebody more frequently or less frequently according to how successfully we have been able to work together. No actual 'dismissal' ever needs to take place if things don't work out well, as I can simply gradually reduce the extent to which I call upon that person's help.

Local communities, once they understand the nature of your project, will sometimes decide for themselves who they consider to be the most appropriate individual, effectively giving you very little choice about who you work with. This arrangement can work well, as the person most likely to be chosen is one whose linguistic knowledge is most highly regarded. In my work on Malakula and Erromango, for example, it has been assumed that I would work extensively with the local Cultural Centre Fieldworkers, and these arrangements have worked well. These are volunteers from within the local community who liaise with the national body that coordinates cultural and linguistic research. They are typically chosen both for their interest in this role, as well as their knowledge of local traditions. Even if there are no individual projects under way in a particular language area, these fieldworkers are given some basic training, equipment, and encouragement to document various aspects of the local culture. When some kind of research project is approved within the local community, there is an expectation that these field workers will be centrally involved in the project, provided with some kind of wage, and also given some kind of further training or experience by the visiting field linguist.

At the same time, there are potential pitfalls in having your language-helper chosen for you. Sometimes, the person who you are expected to work with will be an older member of the community. Such people will typically be good at telling stories, but they may sometimes be less good at paradigmatic elicitation. An older person may also have very prescriptive attitudes toward language. This may get in the way of your desire to be exposed to natural everyday language and it may result in you being exposed only to relatively archaic or formal varieties of the language. Such people may also try to make sure that loanwords which are in everyday use throughout the speech community do not appear in your field notes.

If you are working in a language that is spoken in a town or a city rather than a small rural village, you will almost certainly have more choice about who you are able to work with. You may find it preferable to choose somebody who is closer to yourself in age, temperament, or experience. While in some societies, it may be perfectly acceptable for a man and a woman to work together on a research project, there may be situations in which it is a good idea to match the gender of the researcher and the language-helper, particularly if one or both are unmarried, given the possibility for signals to be misinterpreted in these kinds of situations (Moreno 1995).

It may be that somebody with whom you naturally fall into a friendship ends up more or less spontaneously becoming your language-helper. This way, when you are not actually working, you can be hanging out together, and your ordinary social interactions are likely spontaneously to produce additional linguistic data. For instance, you may be out in the bush together and if you come across trees for which you have not yet recorded names, you can easily add these words to your lexicon.

Similarly, if you are out in a canoe over the reef, there will be fish and other sea creatures for which you will be able to record the names. If your language-helper is an older person, however, he or she may have reduced mobility and is perhaps more likely to sit around at home. This means that the amount of 'after-hours' spontaneous language data that you will be able to record will be less.

While there can be advantages in seeking to match your own age with that of your language-helper, there may be limits on how closely you will be able to do this. If you are a relatively youthful graduate student, members of the community may not view it as appropriate for somebody in their twenties to be the primary—or even the only—source of your linguistic information. One way around this might be to work with a younger person for certain kinds of tasks, such as transcribing stories or making grammaticality judgements, while working with older people who are more respected in the community for tasks such as lexical elicitation, and for the recording of stories.

You may sometimes be expected to work with the very old because of the community's respect for their knowledge and experience. However, older speakers are much more likely to tire easily so there may be real limits to how much time you can work with them. Old people often also have unclear articulation. I have recorded old people whose distinctions between *l* and *n*, or between *l* and *r*, were almost impossible for me to hear. Many Australian languages have phonemic contrasts between dental and alveolar stops, nasals and laterals, but if an elderly speaker no longer has any front teeth, it can be very difficult to work out which sounds are being produced.

I have also found that older people are much less likely to have an ability to recognize paradigms or other grammatical patterns. That is, if you ask someone how to say *I sing*, some people will very quickly learn to also give you the forms for *you sing, (s)he sings, we sing, they sing*, and so on. Older people, however, get very confused by paradigmatic elicitation, and frequently give the incorrect forms. For instance, if you ask how to say *I sing*, some people will actually give you the form for *you sing*, and when you ask for *you sing*, you end up with the form for *I sing* instead. Some older people quickly get bored by the whole process of paradigmatic elicitation, feeling as if they are just repeating the same word over and over. ('I've already told you that word, why are you asking me again?') My experience tells me that it is younger people who are more likely to understand that I am actually asking for different words.

However, the same people who get bored or confused with paradigmatic elicitation may turn out to be excellent providers of vocabulary. Some people seem to have an ability to think up new words that you would never have thought of asking for, and they can provide additional senses of a word that somebody else might not think of. Yet other people often turn out to be particularly good at helping in the transcription and translation of recorded stories, while other people find this tedious and frustrating.

However many people you end up working with, you are going to have to provide them with some clear idea of what it is that you want from each of them as you sit down to work together. While you may be quite familiar with the idea of linguistic elicitation, this is something that your language-helpers will never have been asked to do before. You may therefore need to explain even very basic notions to people, such as the fact that you need them to pronounce sentences slowly, word by word.

When you ask somebody to repeat something, you will need to make it clear that you need an exact repetition of the same thing rather than some kind of a paraphrase. When you are transcribing a text, you will need to make it clear how much text you can handle at a time before you have to play the next section of the story. You will also need to make sure that people repeat exactly what they hear on tape, even where it contains some kind of error. Of course, you will indicate in your notes what the nature of the error was so that this can be corrected in the version that you finally make available to the community.

4.2 Phonological and grammatical elicitation

Social scientists often approach their research projects with 'questionnaires' which they 'administer' to their 'subjects'. Field linguists often do something like this, though we tend to talk instead about 'prompts' which we 'present' to our 'informants' (or, as I have already suggested, 'language-helpers'). That is, you will very often start your data-gathering by saying to somebody with whom you share a common language 'How do you say X in your language?'

4.2.1 Language of elicitation

If the major lingua franca of the area where you are working is English, then you will need to find somebody who speaks English well enough with whom you can use English as your medium of elicitation, at least in the initial stages. In a rural area, this means that your first language-helpers may need to be schoolteachers or other people who have completed more than the minimal amount of formal schooling. If the major lingua franca of the area is not English, you are almost certainly going to have to make a fairly early switch to using whatever that language may be.

If there is a local lingua franca—such as Melanesian Pidgin in the case of the Melanesian countries or Swahili in East Africa—it is possible that this language will be typologically more similar to the local language than English is. This means that the lingua franca may make more of the same kinds of semantic and grammatical distinctions that are made in the local language you are studying. English, for instance, does not have separate inclusive and exclusive pronouns in the first person plural, using the form *we* for both situations. In Melanesian Pidgin, there is a systematic distinction between inclusive *yumi* and exclusive *mifala,* and this distinction mirrors what we find in practically all of the Oceanic languages of Melanesia. In eliciting verbal paradigms, therefore, it is often going to be much easier to operate through the medium of Melanesian Pidgin than English, even if your language-helper speaks perfectly good English.

Sometimes, of course, your own knowledge of the local lingua franca may not yet be up to the task of elicitation, and you may not be able to find a single person who speaks English. In this rather unfortunate kind of situation, you will have no option but to start the process of elicitation using an interpreter. This means that you will need to find somebody who you can communicate with in English or some other language, and who also knows enough of another language that local people know so that your questions can be translated. You will then be able to transcribe the response of the local person.

I, as somebody who speaks no Spanish, could therefore engage somebody who speaks Spanish and English to interview somebody else who speaks Spanish and Zapotec in order for me to work on Zapotec. It does not take much imagination to see that this would not be a very satisfactory way of doing fieldwork, at least in the long term. It is well known that a competent bilingual ability does not automatically equate to an ability to translate, and messages can easily get confused in the process of transmission. This process requires that both the interpreter and the language-helper grasp the point of my question. The merest hint of ambiguity or lack of clarity at any point becomes the weak point in the chain, as the children's game of Chinese Whispers clearly illustrates.

Ultimately, you may want to move towards monolingual elicitation in which you learn enough of the local language to be able to speak directly to your language-helper in that language. Some linguists become very confident at gathering information this way, while others continue to elicit through the medium of the local lingua franca.

4.2.2 Working environment

You should try to organize a place in which you can work comfortably with somebody while you are gathering your data. You will of course need to operate within the limits of what is available locally, unless you have been able to bring your own office furniture with you. For personal comfort, you will need a table with a smooth surface of the right working height, a stable chair with a comfortable back, good light, and good protection from the sun and rain.

However, you can't always get what you want, so you may sometimes end up balancing your notebook on your knee while you are sitting on a log or an upturned canoe. Make sure then, that you come prepared with a firm clipboard, or that you have a notebook with a hard cover. If the tables and chairs are made within the community, you may simply have to make do with a wobbly table that is uncomfortably low or high, or a stool without a back. If the place that you are expected to work in is a poorly ventilated galvanized iron building in which it is hot enough to bake a loaf of bread any time after 11.00 a.m., you will have to learn to write in such a way that your forearm does not drip sweat all over the page that you are about to write on. If your working conditions are less than ideal, don't try to push yourself beyond your physical limits, as you are not going to be much use to anybody with a sore back or a semi-permanent crick in your neck.

You also need to find somewhere to work that is reasonably quiet and private. You may find that your activities attract all manner of interest, and people may end up standing around watching. If you are an exhibitionist, this may be fine, but I find myself wanting to scream after just a short period of being stared at while I'm trying to work. Also, if you've just heard a word and you can't quite decide if the vowel was long or short and you ask for it to be repeated, you risk getting half a dozen other people repeating the word at not quite the same time, which is practically no help at all. If young children are your main audience, you can probably get rid of them fairly quickly, but if you are attracting an audience of adults, this can be more difficult to achieve without causing offence.

4.2.3 Initial elicitation

A field linguist should always begin a session of work by preparing enough questions to last for two or three hours. To prepare yourself, you will need to go over your previous notes so that you have a good idea of the kinds of things that are likely to be interesting, or which still represent problems in your analysis. It is not a good idea to come to an elicitation session with a blank sheet with the intention of just thinking of things to ask as you go along. From time to time, you are likely to get stuck for something to ask, and as you sit there thinking, your language-helper is likely to be getting bored. A bored language-helper very easily becomes distracted, and this is where mistakes are often made.

It is a good idea not to aim to work with somebody for more than a couple of hours at a time, or maybe three hours at the outside. Beyond this length of time, I find that language-helpers tend to get bored, and I have already indicated that this can easily lead to mistakes being made. In fact, I find that much more than two or three hours at a stretch is about all I can cope with myself, especially if my working environment is in any way uncomfortable. This then gives you plenty of time in the same day to analyse the data that you have gathered, and to plan your next session of elicitation.

Elicitation should normally begin with some basic vocabulary, i.e. words that are going to be easy to gather, and which are likely to involve the smallest number of grammatical mysteries. The standard Swadesh 200-word list is a good place to start (Samarin 1967: 220), but there is no reason why you should not veer away from this in your vocabulary elicitation if people seem interested in providing additional words in particular semantic domains. This basic wordlist was also compiled as a non-culture-specific list, so there are likely to be additional words that relate to local culture, as well as the local environment, that you can elicit very early on. Your primary purpose at this initial stage is not really the recording of vocabulary as such, as it is highly likely that at least some of your lexical material at this early stage will contain errors of various kinds. Ultimately, all of the lexical data you record in the early stages will need to be properly checked again for phonetic, semantic, and grammatical accuracy.

One of the first basic lessons in elicitation should be, 'Never tell your language-helper that he/she has given the wrong answer.' Always write down what somebody tells you, even if it is obvious to you that it is not the answer to the question that you asked. The reason for the error may be your language-helper's, for mishearing or misunderstanding your question. However, your own knowledge of the intermediary language may not be nearly as good as you think it is, resulting in your question being unclear. If the answer that you have just written down was not the one you wanted, you should try asking for the same information in a different way.

Your primary purpose in the initial stages of linguistic elicitation is to formulate working hypotheses regarding the phonological system of the language, i.e. what sorts of phonemic contrasts are made, and what phonetic differences represent conditioned or free variants of the same phoneme. You will also be looking for patterns relating to the phonotactic system of the language, i.e. can words contain consonant clusters? If so, what kinds of clusters are permitted? Are clusters permitted only between vowels, or do they also occur at the beginnings of words and ends of words? These (and many more) questions are the kinds of things that should be going through your mind at this initial stage of lexical elicitation.

The first few sessions with a speaker of a language will often sort out most issues of phonemic analysis for most languages, with perhaps a relatively small number of problems emerging as areas worthy of closer attention once you manage to accumulate more data. The best advice at this stage would be to suspend the search for solutions on some of these less immediately tractable problems until you've done some work on some of the other more basic aspects of the language. Some of these kinds of problems end up solving themselves anyway when other kinds of data come in.

When you are carrying out your initial vocabulary elicitation, it is a good idea to start with terms for body parts and the names of things that you can see around you in your immediate vicinity, such as the heavens, the ocean, the rivers, and the land. As I stated earlier, the aim should be to operate with vocabulary in the early stage of elicitation that involves few possibilities of grammatical complexity. Body parts, for instance, may sometimes turn out to be an inappropriate area to concentrate on in elicitation if it turns out that there is obligatory marking of inalienable possession. Verbs are often best avoided in the initial sessions because there may be obligatory marking of inflectional categories such as subject and/or object, as well as tense/aspect/mood.

For many languages, the fieldworker will probably have gained a reasonable idea of what constitutes the set of phonemic contrasts when something like 300–400 words have been elicited. If there are still some remaining mysteries, you could expand your vocabulary with a few more sessions of lexical elicitation to see if this adds enough additional information. Of course, it may be that for some languages, the phoneme inventory is much more complicated, in which case you are likely to have to gather a much larger working vocabulary before you can be at all confident about the set of phonemic contrasts.

No doubt you will at some stage want to check on what look like minimal pairs in your growing corpus of lexical data. You may want to pronounce these pairs of words yourself and ask your language-helper if you have pronounced them correctly. There is a real risk, however, in doing this, as simply being able to understand what you have said, no matter how badly you have mauled the sounds, may be sufficient to warrant a positive response. It is always far better to get your language-helper to repeat what he thinks you have said so that you can check to see if that matches up with what you were attempting to say in the first place.

4.2.4 Eliciting grammatical patterns

Once your phoneme inventory looks reasonably secure, you could then start moving on to the elicitation of grammatical data. You could start by testing for the existence of different possessive patterns by asking for some of the nouns that you have already elicited, but asking how people would express these with noun and pronoun possessors. That is, if you already have asked the word for *canoe*, ask how to say *my canoe* and *the boy's canoe*. Once you start eliciting paradigms like this, it is important that you elicit the full paradigm in case some parts of the paradigm exhibit particular patterns of morphological behaviour. This means that you should not ask for just *my canoe*, but also *your (sg) canoe, his/her canoe, our canoe*, and so on.

In my experience, once you start working on grammatical patterns, it becomes necessary to vary what you are doing during your sessions. When you are eliciting vocabulary, you are likely to be asking for words in closely related semantic fields all together, e.g. body parts, trees, fish, and so on. However, people are less likely to recognize from a whole series of sentence prompts that you are interested in the expression of the past tense, conditional constructions, relative clauses, and so on. If, during your elicitation session, you notice the tell-tale signs that your language-helper is suffering from boredom or nicotine withdrawal (or if you are), then by all means break off your elicitation and relax for a few minutes before getting back into the swing of things, perhaps from a slightly different direction.

You could perhaps start looking at what sorts of categories are marked on verbs, as there may be obligatory subject affixes, or object affixes, or tense/aspect/mood affixes. So, you could ask for simple sentences such as *My canoe is sinking, My canoe sank, My canoe will sink*, and so on. You could quickly move on to negative constructions by asking for sentences such as *Your canoe will not sink* and *Their canoe did not sink*. Again, it is important as far as possible to elicit full paradigms for each verb for all of the categories that are associated with each verb in case there are regular allomorphic variants to be found among any of the verbal suffixes or prefixes.

As soon as you start eliciting pronominal paradigms of this sort, you need to be aware of the kinds of confusion that can arise between the prompt of the field linguist and the response of your language-helper. Some people, when asked for the word (or phrase) for *my eye* will translate literally what the linguist has said. Other people, when presented with the same prompt, will instead give the equivalent of *your eye*. This kind of thing can cause confusion for the fieldworker, which you will need to sort out. Ideally, you should not attempt to correct your language-helper. Instead, you should simply note down anything that he or she says, and if something that is said later seems to contradict what was said earlier, you could try asking the same question all over again to see what sort of response you get.

Once you think that you have sorted out some of the basic patterns of obligatory inflectional marking on nouns or verbs, you will be ready to begin the elicitation of slightly more elaborate sentences. You will need to establish what the basic constituent order of the sentence is, i.e. whether the language is an SVO language, or if it exhibits some other kind of pattern. To do this, you can present simple sentences for translation, such as:

The man saw the dog.
The dog ate the meat.

As far as possible, you should stick with words that you have already elicited when asking people for these kinds of sentences. It is also a good idea to ask people to translate only those kinds of sentences that they are ever likely to need to say in the language. Since kangaroos are herbivores, it therefore makes little sense to ask a speaker of an Australian language how they would say *The kangaroo ate the wallaby*. If you need to elicit the verbal object form of the word for *wallaby*, use it in association with another verb that makes much more sense, such as *The kangaroo saw the wallaby*.

It may also be necessary to work out what sorts of meanings are unlikely ever to be expressed for cultural reasons. For example, there are societies in which the following is unlikely ever to be said:

The man wove a mat with his mother-in-law.

People may be unlikely to say a sentence like this for a number of reasons. If only women traditionally make mats, you would be unlikely to need to speak of a man who is weaving a mat. If mats are always made by a single person, it may make little sense to speak of two people working together on a mat. Finally, if a man and his mother-in-law are governed by social rules that prevent them from sitting together in such close proximity, the two of them would be unlikely to appear together in a single sentence of this type.

Finally, you should stick to words and activities in your sentences that you know people will have readily accepted words for in their language. For many languages, it would not make much sense to start eliciting grammatical patterns with sentences such as the following:

The student booted up the computer.

This is because in many parts of the world, this kind of meaning is likely to be expressed using ad hoc loans from a language of wider communication rather than words from the local language.

While this is a very obvious example, there are other examples that are perhaps less obvious. When I was eliciting vocabulary in Paamese, I asked people for the word for 'get married', which I wrote down. Then I asked the word for 'get divorced'. The response was a brief pensive look, followed by the comment:

We don't get divorced.

When you are investigating the grammar, you will need to find out how a range of additional information is encoded in the simple sentence, such as how peripheral semantic roles are expressed. You will therefore need to present English prepositional and adverbial phrases for translation, such as the following:

The man saw the dog in the river.
The dog ate the meat under the house.
The man will see the dog tomorrow.
The dog died because of the poison.

Finally, you will be able to move on to the elicitation of a range of complex sentence constructions. You would therefore start asking for the equivalents of relative clauses, e.g.

The man saw the dog which swam across the river.

or other kinds of subordinate clauses, e.g.

The dog swam across the river because it was hungry.
The dog drowned when it tried to swim across the river.
If the dog swims across the river, it might drown.

You would also need to elicit coordinate sentence patterns, e.g.

The dog swam across the river and the man spoke to his son.
The dog swam across the river but the man spoke to his son.

If I thought it might be practical to provide a universal elicitation schedule which any fieldworker could work through in order to analyse the grammar of any language, I would be happy to include this as part of this guide to fieldwork. However, I think that this would be of only limited value. Of much greater value are elicitation schedules that have been designed specifically for languages in certain geographical or genetic groupings (e.g. Samarin 1967: 110, Bouquiaux and Thomas 1992). Of course, once you become aware of the structural features that are commonly encountered in the language family that you are working on, you may even be in a position to draw up a basic elicitation schedule yourself.

Any intending fieldworker needs to survey the literature for closely related languages to find out what kinds of patterns are found in those languages and what sorts of constructions are absent. For somebody who is intending to work on an Australian language, it is essential to know that in these languages there is often just a single possessive construction for all kinds of possessive relationships, while in Oceanic languages, there are often distinct possessive constructions depending on the nature of the precise relationship between the possessor and the thing possessed. Thus, the direction of your elicitation needs to be guided by patterns that are revealed in your background reading for related languages.

4.2.5 Taking notes

When you elicit data in the kinds of ways that I have been talking about, there are essentially two different ways of keeping a record of what people say. On the one hand, you can simply write everything down in a notebook. Alternatively, you can use your audio recorder in much the same way as a notebook by recording every response. When I first started doing fieldwork on Australian languages, I recorded pretty well everything on tape. Anybody listening to those tapes in the archive will therefore hear my prompt, followed by the response from the speaker of whatever language I was recording at the time. I then transcribed these tapes in full and my deposited 'field notes' are held in an archive in handwriting that I have never since been able to match in terms of tidiness.

There are advantages in this kind of approach. In the case of the moribund languages that I was working on at the time, we now have an extensive record of the pronunciation of all of the words and individual sentences that I recorded, and future linguists no longer have to rely solely on my transcriptions of that material. However, if you are constantly switching the recorder on and off as you elicit, you are likely to distract your language-helper to some extent. You are also likely to make it more difficult to take notes while you are recording. If you were to record your language-helper's responses directly into a notebook, you could much more easily make little notes to yourself, offering possible alternative transcriptions and points to check, while also noting down interesting asides from your language-helper.

While some linguists continue to make extensive use of audio recordings, these days I use only notebooks for recording responses in direct elicitation sessions. Of course, my notebooks are a horror for anybody else to look at because they contain hurried handwriting as I try to keep up with the rapidity of somebody's speech, and there are scribbled notes relating to all manner of interesting side observations. At the moment, my notebooks are all locked away in a storage cupboard to which only I have access, and I am not sure that I would ever want them to go into a public archive.

Sometimes, a fieldworker's notebooks may even point to aspects of his or her personality or behaviour that are best kept private. I remember reading through some of the original handwritten notebooks of one amateur linguist who recorded valuable data from a large number of Australian languages in the late 1800s and early 1900s. Most of these languages no longer have any speakers and these notebooks, and the resulting publications, represent the only information that we will ever have.

Interestingly, the original notebooks occasionally contained information that was excluded from the final publications, such as words with glosses like 'the sound of bellies slapping during sexual intercourse'. Of course, we can only guess at the circumstances under which such a word could have been elicited, but it would not be difficult for anybody's personal predilections to make their way into a notebook in this way, only to be filtered out in the final selection of published examples.

4.2.6 Native-speaker judgements

Once you get beyond the introductory stages, you will need to begin testing hypotheses about patterns that you should be beginning to formulate in your own mind as you go. This can be done by presenting forms to a speaker and asking for a judgement as to the correctness or otherwise of that form. However, there can be problems associated with this kind of introspective method of data-gathering and such judgements should only be accepted when there is corroborative evidence, either in the form of spontaneous utterances of the same type, or consistently made judgements from several different elicitation sessions, or similar judgements from several speakers. This means that you should not place too much faith in a single grammaticality judgement from a single speaker on a single occasion.

One major problem in presenting forms for judgement in this way is that your notion of 'grammaticality' can very easily be confused with the speaker's notion of 'understandability'. That is, if what you have said is understandable, your language-helper might say that what you have said is OK. It is not always easy to ensure that this kind of judgement corresponds to what people would actually say. Fieldworkers, when they later find out that sentences that were earlier given the OK are in reality ungrammatical, have been informed in terms such as the following: *Well, you can say that, but we wouldn't.* Or: *That's alright, but it's not really what we say.* Any comment like that should be taken as a warning that you are possibly on the wrong track with your elicitation strategy. So, you should avoid strategies such as the following in your elicitation sessions:

Is X grammatical?
Can you say X?

Rather, you should formulate your elicitation sessions with questions more like the following:

Would people say X?

It is also going to be very difficult for you to control for all possible variables when you present a sentence in isolation for a grammaticality judgement like this. A simple change in intonation—which you may be completely unaware of—may completely change the acceptability of an utterance within any particular real-world context. Thus, somebody may respond that your prompt is incorrect (or that it is correct), but you and your language-helper may be thinking about quite different real-world contexts in which this would be the case.

One way of giving grammaticality judgements greater reliability is to present people with two (or more) options and to allow them to indicate which they think is the better sentence. Thus, rather than any of the strategies above, it may be a better idea to ask somebody:

Which is better: X or Y?

When you are eliciting sentences, and perhaps more so when you are transcribing texts, you are likely from time to time to encounter a pattern that you simply do not understand. Maybe a completely new morpheme has appeared in your notes for the first time, or maybe a morpheme which you thought you understood perfectly suddenly appears in a context which does not fit with what you had come to expect. No doubt you will give a little pause, furrow your brow, and you will want to ask your language-helper:

Why did you say X rather than Y?

Very often, the answer to this kind of question calls for much greater linguistic sophistication than any linguistically untrained language-helper is going to be in a position to provide.

My advice to the fieldworker is to ask this kind of question just once. If you are lucky enough to have a language-helper who is intuitively gifted in explaining patterns of language, then by all means continue to ask these sorts of questions. But you need to understand that in response to this kind of question, most people are just going to say something unhelpful like the following:

We say it that way because that's the way we say it.

Further reading: Bouquiaux and Thomas (1992: 3–70), Hale (2001: 81–95), Mithun (2001), Samarin (1967: 106–50, 175–204).

4.3 Gathering words

The grammatical system of a language is something that is far more circumscribed than the vocabulary of a language. While writing a grammar can be challenging enough, as well as time-consuming, it can be much more difficult to compile a substantial dictionary of a language. We see this difference reflected in the number of published grammars of languages in comparison to published dictionaries of the same languages. Some of the most widely cited published grammars have no corresponding published dictionaries. This is no doubt in part because some linguists see the lexicographer's work as that of Samuel Johnson's 'harmless drudge', which is beneath their dignity. But I have little doubt that part of the reason is also that there is simply far too much work involved if the job is to be done at all well.

4.3.1 Direct elicitation

I have already described how you can start a lexical compilation for a language by directly eliciting vocabulary via another language. You should always ensure that you elicit vocabulary in semantic fields rather than running through a list that is organized alphabetically in, say, English. If you have a list of words that some other linguist has gathered in the language that you are working on and you want to check these forms for accuracy, you should again try to put the words together in semantic groupings first, rather than presenting words to somebody in what will seem like random order if they are listed alphabetically. There are some useful wordlists that you may want to get hold of before setting out for fieldwork: for example, in Australia there is Sutton and Walsh (1979), and more generally, but with an African focus, is Bouquiaux and Thomas (1992). Similar elicitation aids can be found for other regions.

Although body parts represent one of the easiest semantic fields in which to elicit vocabulary, you need to be careful not to try to elicit names for *all* body parts at the very beginning of the relationship with your language-helper. I have found that the initial stage of elicitation in a new language sometimes attracts an audience, which makes the occasion a very public one. I therefore tend to skip straight from navel to knee when eliciting body parts if there are other people around. This is because words for any of the intermediate body parts may cause embarrassment if men or women do not use these words in each other's presence in public. In fact, there may be even more at issue here than embarrassment because in some societies, the use of certain words may be completely taboo in the presence of particular relatives. You can always wait till your relationship with your language-helper becomes relaxed enough that you can ask for these kinds of words in private.

You should be warned that these kinds of restrictions may not apply just to the names of body parts between the navel and the knee. Mention of certain cultural items, for example, may also need to be avoided in public, though it may be more difficult to predict what cannot be mentioned, and when. On one occasion, I was eliciting vocabulary for a number of cultural items which were described in an ethnographic account of one society. I was working with an adult man but a number of young boys came to sit and quietly listen to what we were doing. The two of us had earlier been talking about the bullroarers that are used to make a frightening noise when boys are being circumcised. I had forgotten to write down the name at the time so I asked what it was again. My answer was a quick kick in the shin under the table. I immediately realized that this was a surprise that still awaited the boys in the audience and had to delay my question to a more opportune moment.

It can sometimes be helpful to elicit vocabulary with small groups of people rather than in one-on-one sessions with a single language-helper. It can be remarkably easy for somebody on their own to be unable to think of a translation equivalent for even a fairly basic vocabulary item, but another person will often be able to step in straight away with the appropriate word. When one person says one word, this may also remind some of the other people present of other related words. People in groups can sometimes also find additional senses to words in discussion which might not necessarily occur to somebody working singly with a linguist.

While group sessions like this can be a productive way to work, you need to be aware that there can sometimes be a downside as well. One of my language-helpers on Malakula once decided that it would be a good idea to call for a meeting of interested people one Sunday after-noon to help sort out some vocabulary relating to specific aspects of the traditional culture. Something like fifteen or twenty people turned up. Things were not run as a formal meeting, so people sat around and contributed when they wanted to, and they listened (and occasionally dozed) when they had nothing to contribute. The problem was that every time I wanted to check that I had transcribed a word correctly and I asked somebody to repeat it, I would tend to get repetitions from several people at once, meaning that I heard nobody's repetition properly. Try as I could, people did not seem to understand why I would only want *one* person to repeat the word if I had called a public meeting of many people.

4.3.2 Beyond elicitation

Accumulating vocabulary simply by asking for translation equivalents from the language of elicitation is going to come up against a blank after a certain point. This is because many English words will not necessarily have convenient equivalents in another language. There will similarly be many words in the other language that do not have direct equivalents in English. For instance, you would probably only come across a word meaning something like 'arrive on the scene just as somebody is talking about you' in a text, as you would almost certainly not think to ask for such a word if you were getting translation equivalents from English. Even if you did happen to think to ask for such a word, there is no guarantee that any given individual would be able to think of that particular word in response to such a prompt. Another issue related to the direct elicitation of vocabulary involves the extended senses of a particular word. While you might manage to elicit a word with a particular meaning, your language-helper may not immediately think of any of the extended senses of the word.

Any time that you see something new, you can ask what that thing is called. The easiest way to find new names for trees is to take a notebook with you every time you go into the bush with somebody. Every time you see somebody doing something new, you can ask somebody to say what they are doing. Sometimes these items or these activities may not be 'lexicalized', i.e. there may not be a unique word to express that particular meaning, but sometimes there may be and you will be in a position to record it.

This kind of approach means that you should always remember to have a pen and a pocket notebook with you. I have been known to forget and it then becomes necessary to become creative in finding ways to remind yourself of the new words that you have recovered. I was once in the bush with some people who taught me some new words that I did not want to forget, so I ended up scratching the words onto the husk of a green coconut with a knife. Of course, I then had to face the inconvenience of carrying that coconut with me for the rest of the day, or risk forgetting those words. Of course, there are going to be times when you won't be able to have your pen and notebook with you. I suspect that my own lexical collections relating to creatures living on the sea floor are less rich than they could be for this very reason.

Another way in which you could add to your stock of words is to get people working in brainstorming groups dealing with particular topics. That is, perhaps you could encourage one group of people to work together to come up with as many names of different kinds of trees as they can think of. Another group could be working on fish, and another group could be thinking of names of different kinds of birds. There could be a large number of different groups of people working on a wide variety of words belonging to particular semantic fields, such as terms involved in house-building, the construction of canoes, the weaving of mats and baskets, and so on. The advantage of having people working in particular semantic fields like this is that one word may easily lead to another word in the same area.

There may be illustrated books which you can also use as prompts to elicit vocabulary. In many parts of the world, there is a variety of publications dealing with local flora and fauna and people may be able to provide names of trees, plants, birds, fish, animals, and insects from the pictures that are contained in these volumes. However, there are often limitations to the usefulness of books such as these as aids to elicitation. For one thing, people sometimes find it difficult to recognize individual species when presented with a small illustration, especially if there is no indication of what other species are found nearby as part of the normal environment in which that species is found. Sometimes, while there may be a visual clue distinguishing one species from another, it may be that the vital distinction in the mind of speakers of some languages depends on one of our other senses. For instance, people may distinguish one tree from another by the smell of its bark or its flowers, or they may distinguish one bird from another by their song, or by the kind of nests that they make.

It must also be remembered that speakers of languages do not necessarily classify the world in the same way that botanists and zoologists classify things. This means that sometimes different species that are similar in particular ways may actually be referred to by the same term. Sometimes, different varieties of the same species may also have different names with no generic name for the overall species. Another possibility is that people may have quite different names for the same species depending on the stage of growth it is at.

4.3.3 Spontaneous speech

While various strategies of direct elicitation can certainly help in the search for new vocabulary, it is extremely important that elicitation be supplemented by an extensive collection of spoken texts. I have already indicated that the recording of texts is essential for a detailed understanding of the grammar of a language, as well as for understanding how sentences are linked together in discourse. But these same texts will also contain a huge amount of very valuable lexical information. You will find that in the first such texts that you transcribe, you will encounter many new lexical items, as well as many examples of words that are used with previously unrecorded secondary senses. You may also encounter a range of words which appear in new idiomatic constructions.

The more texts you are able to record the better, and the more varied these texts are in terms of content, the more new words you are likely to discover. I have also found myself happy to agree to record somebody telling the same story that somebody else has already told because it is most unlikely that two people talking about the same topic will use exactly the same range of vocabulary.

However, by the time that you have recorded a certain amount of speech, each individual text will provide fewer and fewer new pieces of new lexical information, except perhaps for texts that deal with specialized knowledge of some kind. Before too long, you may find that each individual text may provide you with just one or two new pieces of information. The Law of Diminishing Returns comes into effect here. At some point, you need to ask yourself whether the massive task of recording new texts and then transcribing them is worth the relatively small amount of new lexical data that you are likely to discover.

Of course, once you encounter any new word in a text, you can then take that as an opportunity to present the word to people for another brainstorming session to see if they can come up with any other words that are related to it in the same semantic field. You can also question people to see if these new words have any extended senses.

A good fieldworker will also have his or her ears open all the time as people are speaking in the daily round. People will often use words and expressions that you have never heard before and these should be noted down immediately. Whenever you record a new word in this way, though, you should be sure to check it later either with somebody who was taking part in the original conversation, or with somebody else. You will need to remember that your own knowledge of the language is not that of a native speaker. No matter how well you think you know the language, your knowledge will still be far short of how well local people know it, and it is surprisingly easy to mishear a word, or to misunderstand what somebody has said. If you cannot independently verify a word that you *think* you heard in conversation, then it is probably safer to assume that you misheard it.

4.3.4 Sound substitutions

Another way to look for possible new words would be to adopt the sound substitution method. By this method, you could start with all of the words that you have already recorded and invent a complete set of possible minimal pairs involving all of the phonemic contrasts in the language. Thus, if you have already recorded a word of the shape *pali*, you could ask people if they know of the word *pari*, or *pati*, or *padi*, and so on. Of course, other sounds could be substituted so you could also present people with prompts such as *bali*, *dali*, and *tali*, as well as *pili* and *puli*, and so it goes.

Some linguists have gone to the trouble of taking the various segments in the phoneme inventory, as well as a statement of the phonotactics which governs the possible shapes of words, to provide a printout of all of the logically possible words in the language. It would then be necessary to go carefully through this list of potential words with speakers of a language to cross out all of the nonsense words, and then to assign meanings to those forms which people recognize as genuine words in the language. The problem with these last two approaches is that they could easily become very boring, both for the linguist and for your language-helpers. A bored language-helper is likely to be a distracted language-helper, and this is when errors are likely to start creeping in.

Let me show you something of the nature of the problem with an imaginary language. A language might have five vowels *i*, *e*, *a*, *o*, and *u*, and fifteen consonants *p*, *t*, *k*, *b*, *d*, *g*, *m*, *n*, *ŋ*, *f*, *s*, *h*, *l*, and *r*, and it might have the simplest phonotactic pattern possible, with syllables consisting of any consonant followed by any single vowel, and words could be one, two, or three syllables long. With these fifteen consonants and five vowels, there would be 75 possible monosyllabic words. There would be 5,625 possible disyllabic words, and there would be 421,875 possible trisyllabic words. Since a dictionary that contains 25,000 entries would ordinarily be considered a fairly substantial piece of work, this means that people would be expected to eliminate over 400,000 nonsense words.

It is hard to imagine anybody having the patience to stick with such a mind-numbingly boring task. If one person were to do nothing but cross off non-existing words from such a list after thirty seconds of thought for each word, and that person worked for eight hours a day, five days a week, the task would not be finished until just over one year and eight months later . . . and that is assuming no time off for annual leave, illness, or lunch and coffee breaks! This is clearly not a wise path to follow.

4.3.5 When is the dictionary done?

At some stage, you are going to have to ask yourself when your dictionary might be 'complete'. Any decision about when to stop collecting new words and to start the process of writing up the dictionary is necessarily going to be somewhat arbitrary, as there will never be a time when you can say that you have finally recorded the 'last' word in a language. Not only is the vocabulary of every language absolutely enormous, but vocabularies are constantly changing in any case. I have found that even in very small languages with just a few hundred speakers, after an absence of a year, new slang expressions can become established in the community.

You will be able to record your first 300 or 400 words in just a day or two. You should be able to reach your first thousand words after a week or two of effort, in conjunction with progress that you have made on the grammar and the phonology. In order to reach the 2,000-word stage, you can probably expect to take several months and to have to put in a lot more effort than it took to reach the first thousand words. Getting to 3,000 words may take you a year or so if you are also involved in the writing of a grammar at the same time. Each additional thousand words is going to be increasingly difficult to discover.

There is no single correct answer to the question: How many words should a dictionary contain? There are dictionaries of some local languages which may contain up to 20,000 entries, but these dictionaries have often benefited from a century or more of lexicographical tradition, with the first efforts having been much more modest in scope. If you are the first person to ever write a dictionary of a language and you are working on a grammar of the language at the same time, it would be quite a respectable effort if you could manage a dictionary of between 5,000 and 10,000 words.

Further reading: Hale (2001: 95–8), Samarin (1967: 205–17), Vaux and Cooper (1999: 37–49), Bouquiaux and Thomas (1992: 401–687).

4.4 Keeping track of data

Because the writing of a grammar and a dictionary is likely to be spread out over several years, you are going to have to develop some kind of system for making your information accessible, as well as for keeping it safe. While you are in the field, your methods of data organization may have to be slightly different from what they would be at home where you have an office with a computer and limitless supplies of stationery. However, you will still need to be able to locate important examples in the field without too much trouble, and you will need to be able to recognize the difference between data which is reliable and data which calls for further checking.

4.4.1 Daily records

Anthropological fieldwork tends to revolve around the maintenance of quite elaborate diaries in which the details of each day are laid out for future reference. A linguist clearly does not need to be encumbered by this kind of requirement, though we do still need to keep a linguistically informative record of every piece of information that we observe. I have already referred to the notebooks that you will be working with in the field. It is probably a good idea to have separate notebooks for elicited data, for text transcriptions, and for lexical data. If you end up recording data from more than one language, it would also be extremely wise to have a separate set of notebooks for each language. Including data from more than one language in a single notebook increases the possibility that you may accidentally ascribe forms from one language to a different language.

Whenever you have a working session, it is a good idea to indicate the date, the place, and the name of the person who provided the data. You should also indicate where that person comes from because there may be dialect differences of which you are not yet aware. If you end up with large amounts of data recorded from large numbers of people, you at some point have to decide about the reliability of one piece of information vis-à-vis some other piece of information. The date of recording may be relevant, as older information may be less reliable than information that you have gathered more recently. The specific person who provided the information may also be relevant if you eventually come to realize that certain people are more likely than others to get confused about certain kinds of things that you ask for.

If you are eliciting data by having somebody translate from a lingua franca into the local language, it is a good idea to prepare your prompts fully ahead of time in your notebook. Be sure to leave plenty of space in relation to each example so that you can clearly indicate whether your language-helper found the sentence acceptable or not. Your language-helper may also spontaneously offer alternative ways of saying the same thing. It is a good idea to record such information as well, so allow space for this.

When I am transcribing texts, I typically transcribe with two or three lines of free space beneath each line of text. This allows me space to provide any kind of translation notes as I go on another line to the actual text. I also transcribe onto only a single page of my notebook, leaving the other page blank. This means that I can use that page for any kind of further grammatical or lexical elicitation that might occur to me while I am doing the transcription. Using different pages clearly distinguishes the elicited material from the transcribed material.

4.4.2 Filing systems

Some guides to fieldwork (e.g. Samarin 1967) advocate quite extensive systems of data-filing in the field so that individual examples of a wide variety of structural patterns can be easily located. I have never managed to summon the dedication or find the opportunity to develop such an elaborate system of card-filing for grammatical data, so I would suggest that unless you really cannot find your way around your corpus, the amount of work involved in putting such a system together in the field might be better spent on more elicitation and more text transcription. It is probably going to be a better idea to leave such detailed organization of your data until you return home where you can make use of sophisticated electronic systems of filing such as *Toolbox*.

With regard to lexical data, there is a variety of ways in which information can be recorded in the field. One of these ways could be called the *page-filing* method. Just as the name suggests, this is a method of keeping track of information that involves putting words onto pages in a book. If you can find a solid notebook in which sections are marked by letters of the alphabet, this would be a good addition to your fieldwork kitbag. If you can't find such a notebook, you could of course always add your own tags to show where you can find words beginning with *A*, *B*, and so on.

There is a variety of ways in which you can organize your lexical data in notebooks in the field. It might be a good idea if you keep all words referring to trees together in a single place, and all words referring to birds. You might also want to keep all of your verbs together in a single place, perhaps even having separate places for your transitive verbs and your intransitive verbs.

Within each of these groups you can organize your information alphabetically to make it easier for you to find your way through these lists later when you are looking for a particular word. Of course, when you start out on such a notebook, you should leave plenty of lines between your early entries to allow for subsequent entries to be placed in appropriate alphabetical order. It would also be a good idea to leave several blank pages between each different section of your notebook to allow for expansion in the number of entries within each section.

When you have collected a large number of items, however, you are likely to find it difficult to keep things in strict alphabetical order because items are not 'movable' once you have entered them in your book. If you were to write items in pencil, you could erase them and move them down the page to make space for a newly inserted item above it. You could also write entries in pen but use white-out to shift an item down the page. However, this is not a good idea, especially if you end up using white-out over white-out, because eventually this can crack and break off and you will lose all or part of whatever was written there.

While some of us may have wonderfully tidy handwriting, this is certainly not true for all of us. With my handwriting, I sometimes find that written *v* and *r* look remarkably similar. I am unlikely to find it too much of a problem trying to work out whether a word should be *van* or *ran* in English, as the context is likely to provide me with relevant clues. There has therefore been relatively little motivation for me to tidy up this aspect of my handwriting. However, when I am recording lexical data by hand in the field, I have *often* been uncertain later as to whether I had intended to write a *v* or an *r*. If you are entering lexical data by hand, you will need to be aware of any potential confusion in your own handwriting and to compensate for this in your notebook entries. I could compensate for my own tendency to confuse *r* and *v*, for example, by writing such words *extremely* carefully. Alternatively, if I still do not trust myself to distinguish these letters, then I could perhaps write these words in capitals rather than lower case, where this kind of confusion would not be possible.

Another way of organizing lexical data in the field is to use a *card-filing* system. By this method, each separate entry is written on a separate small card. As you find additional words, new words can be inserted in the correct alphabetical order. These cards can be kept in a simple shoebox or in a specially made cabinet of some kind, and the information that is contained on each card can ultimately be transferred to a printed page. Each individual card will be large enough that a number of different kinds of information can easily be included for each word. You can therefore include information about word class membership, as well as examples of sentences in which that word appears.

While your cards are probably best kept in alphabetical order, it is relatively easy for you to pull out all of your words referring to trees, or all of your intransitive verbs, if you wanted to do some kind of testing on these subsets of words. You could make this easier by using cards of different colours for different kinds of words: green cards for trees, pink cards for animals and birds, blue cards for fish, and so on. Of course, once you've pulled all of the cards out for a particular category, it is no major problem to put them back into alphabetical order again.

Although card-filing has its advantages, there are some disadvantages too. The cards that you can buy in stationery stores under the names *index cards* or *system cards* are more like thin cardboard than ordinary paper. This has the advantage of making them durable, but it also makes them relatively expensive to buy in large quantities. It also makes them quite heavy, and therefore potentially expensive to transport, particularly if you were anticipating the recording of 5,000 lexical entries on 5,000 different cards.

Of course, you would also need something to keep your cards in. While shoeboxes are good for keeping larger cards in, if you keep smaller cards in a shoebox, you will find that they will move around in the box and they will easily get out of order. The smallest cards would therefore probably need to be kept in a special drawer, rather like the old-fashioned library catalogue drawers that we used to use before catalogue information was fully digitized.

When I first went to Paama, I took a large bunch of small index cards with me and I kept them in a two-drawer metal box. The box itself was not all that cheap, but that was not the major problem that I faced with it. Being metal, it was also quite bulky and heavy, hence expensive and inconvenient to transport. It certainly was not something that I could carry with me to different people's houses when I wanted to record new vocabulary.

Another disadvantage of a card file like this, in comparison to lexical material that is stored in a notebook, is that you can drop a notebook, pick it up again, and continue along your way after dusting off the cover. But I once had the misfortune to drop my card file. The drawers flung open and a couple of thousand cards all dropped out onto the ground. It then took me several hours to collect all of the cards up and to make sure that I had put them all back correctly in alphabetical order.

I kept that metal card box for many years out of a sense of sentimental attachment, even after I had abandoned all of the cards with the Paamese lexical information on them when I finally produced the published version of the dictionary. It started to rust after many years in the tropics and the drawers became hard to open. I eventually threw it out, and I have never missed the horrible rusty grey monster.

4.4.3 Computer storage

When you have completed your first fieldtrip and you have had an opportunity to organize your data at home in preparation for your next visit, one of your priorities should be to organize your lexical data. You will of course have access to a computer, so all of the information in your notebooks or on your cards should be carefully transferred to a computer file.

You will then be able to produce a tidy printout of all of your lexical data. When you do this, you should be sure to leave lots of white space, and perhaps also to use double spacing. I typically then spiral-bind my printout and this then becomes my working notebook to which I add my new lexical data on my next fieldtrip. If you leave lots of white space in your printout, you can insert new words by hand while you are in the field. It is also a good idea not to copy the dictionary pages back to back. If you have a white page opposite every page of printed text, this gives you plenty of additional space on which to insert new material.

Then, when you get back home again, it will be a relatively simple matter to insert any new material, or to correct any of your old material on your computer file. Of course, if you are planning any further trips, each updated printout of the lexicon can become the basis of your new lexical notebook. Be sure, though, to include the date of each version on the printout so that you can always tell which information represents an update of which older information.

Some fieldworkers will be in a position to enter data directly onto a computer while they are in the field. If you are fortunate enough to be in this position, then by all means make use of the technology because of the ease with which you will be able to access and organize your information. However, you should keep in mind that there are some risks in doing this. Some information is likely to be more reliable in your mind than other information and there is a very real danger that some fairly tentative information may end up indistinguishable in your computer file from more definitive information. This means that you will need to have some way of clearly marking which information needs further checking and which information you are more certain about. This could be as simple as remembering to key in a question mark after information that needs checking.

In one dictionary that I am currently working on, for example, I have entered words that I have only encountered in a published anthropological source that is almost eighty years old in a different field of the database to distinguish these from entries that I have gathered myself. There are other entries which derive from a wordlist compiled by another linguist but which I know from experience is likely to contain many errors. Where I have not yet been able to check these items, I have entered these into another field. Finally, there are forms from my own data about which I am uncertain for a variety of reasons which I have marked with a query in a separate field. This means that I know that only data which appears in a certain field of the database should be treated as fully reliable.

Further reading: Samarin (1967: 151–74), Austin (2006).

4.5 Archiving

A linguist should go beyond merely documenting a language, as the archiving of any materials gathered is also of considerable importance. While your final grammar and dictionary will hopefully appear in published form, it is likely that much of your textual data, as long as your notes, will not be published as such. However, your text transcriptions, and possibly even your field notes, may contain much valuable data that other linguists in the future may be able to make excellent use of to discuss issues that you have not addressed in your own accounts of the language.

For example, since I published my own grammar of Paamese over twenty years ago (Crowley 1982), I have become aware of many aspects of the language that I would treat differently today. There are also parts of the grammar that I can now see were largely ignored in my earlier description. In particular, the animacy hierarchy (human nouns > non-human living things > inanimate nouns) is involved in a wide variety of grammatical constructions. Thus, for example, whether a noun is or is not marked for plurality is dependent on its position in the animacy hierarchy, with highly animate nouns much more frequently overtly marking plural and inanimate nouns seldom marking plural. I was recently able to quantify these tendencies on the basis of observations of the actual behaviour of nouns in my collection of Paamese texts. There are possibly other features of Paamese grammar that linguists in the future may want to investigate when I am no longer around, but since my full collection of texts has been placed in the national archive in Vanuatu, this should not be a problem.

The importance of archiving is perhaps best illustrated by what happens when data is not properly stored. I have worked on one moribund language in Vanuatu where the local chief informed me that about twenty years earlier another linguist had done some of the same kind of work on that language. He told me the name of that linguist. I was involved in the preparation of a comprehensive publication of all published sources relating to all of the languages in the country (Lynch and Crowley 2001), and I never came across any publications in that linguist's name. In violation of the ethical requirement that the results of linguistic fieldwork be provided back to the local community in some locally understandable form, this linguist also appears not to have supplied copies of anything that he wrote to local people. A search of the national archive for cultural and linguistic materials suggests that this linguist also failed to deposit copies of any of his notes or tapes in that archive. If these potentially valuable materials are still in existence, we have absolutely no idea where they are.

I have also heard too many stories of valuable records of little-known languages, or even of languages which have become extinct, that were once kept in an old office that burnt down or which was destroyed in a cyclone. There are also stories of valuable linguistic records which have simply been lost or misplaced while no copies of these notes had ever been deposited in an archive for safe back-up.

When you make your data available for archiving, you need to keep in mind the fact that some of the data you have recorded may need to be treated in specific ways. Some of your audio recordings or your notes, for example, may involve matters that were told in confidence because they identify particular individuals in ways that should not be made public. Some information may be seen as belonging exclusively to some particular lineage, or to some particular group in society. There may also be information which only women or only men are permitted to know.

Such restricted material should only be deposited in an archive if there are strict provisions in place for determining levels of access to that data. Archivists should be able to devise cataloguing systems which list material as being of 'open' access, which anybody can listen to or read, while other material may be listed as being 'closed'. Such material may then only be accessed with the direct permission of the researcher who deposited the material, or of people holding particular positions in the local community.

A field linguist need not become actively involved in the task of archiving. Any detailed discussion of archiving, then, probably does not belong in a fieldwork manual such as this. However, in this day and age, the field linguist needs to appreciate that the task of archiving is likely to be made easier if any audio or video data is recorded in a format that facilitates digital rather than analogue archiving, as this kind of material is less subject to erosion of quality over time. Such recordings call for the acquisition of special recording equipment. Although this is more expensive than traditional analogue recording equipment, linguists should keep this in mind when submitting applications for funding for field research. Indeed, some funding agencies now require a clear statement from applicants about the type of equipment to be used, the formats in which data will be captured, and where and how the data will be archived.

However, analogue recordings (and even field notebooks where this is relevant) should be copied and presented to an appropriate archive for safekeeping. This serves not just to protect the interests of future generations, but even individual researchers themselves. Notes and tapes can be damaged in anybody's office (or in the field) by any manner of disaster, which could be averted by placing copies for safekeeping in a professionally curated archive.

It is not just notes and unpublished materials which should be presented for archiving. In many countries where research permits are issued for linguistic research, linguists who publish materials arising out of their research are also called upon to provide copies of their publications in an appropriate library or archive. Even if you are aware of no explicit requirement that you do this, linguists should consider it as both common courtesy and an ethical obligation to return copies of all offprints of articles and chapters, as well as copies of all books, to local authorities. Not only does this enable local people to see what you have done with the data that you have been given access to, but it also makes future research easier for subsequent researchers if all work from the area that they plan to work in is held in a single location.

Further reading: Austin (2006). For more information on archiving see the Open Language Archives Community (OLAC) homepage: www.language-archives.org. Another useful source is the Digital Endangered Languages and Musics Archive Network (DELAMAN) page: www.delaman.org

5

Beyond Elicitation

I have already indicated that elicitation can take you only so far in your study of a language. In this chapter, I will be discussing some of the issues that we face when trying to record natural speech.

5.1 The textual corpus

An account of any language needs to be based primarily on a substantial corpus of continuous spontaneous speech. Of course, obtaining such a corpus can present the fieldworker with a variety of problems.

5.1.1 Early corpora

Linguists in the past had no choice but to gather their textual corpora by having speakers of the language dictate their stories while they were transcribed 'live'. Such a process is to be avoided these days, for a variety of reasons. First, it has to be enormously taxing on the linguist. Secondly, in the absence of any recording that can be played back later, any mistranscriptions can never be checked. Thirdly, the manner in which the story is told is almost certainly going to result in a style of speaking that is different in unpredictable ways from ordinary language usage given what must seem like a fairly bizarre process for the language-helper.

Some earlier textual corpora were compiled instead by speakers of the language writing the stories themselves. Franz Boas, for example, trained speakers of some of the Amerindian languages that he worked on so that they could write thousands of pages of oral tradition in their languages. European missionaries developed a writing system for Maori in New Zealand in the early 1800s and taught this to the local people so that they could read the Bible that had just been translated into their language. Maori rapidly became more literate in their own language in the first half of the nineteenth century than European settlers were literate in English. Maori began publishing newspapers in their own language, writing letters to each other, and they also wrote down a huge amount of oral tradition and genealogical information, much of which has survived in manuscript form to the present. Valuable as these kinds of linguistic corpora are, however, it must be remembered that written texts often differ from the natural spoken language in a variety of ways.

5.1.2 The recording of speech

A modern grammar should therefore be based primarily on the spoken form of the language. Before the mass production of reel-to-reel tape recorders in the 1950s, it could be very difficult to obtain this kind of data. The only recording that we have of any of the Tasmanian languages is an almost inaudible—and quite short—stretch of Fanny Cochrane-Smith's voice recorded onto an Edison cylinder in the late 1800s. These days, of course, even reel-to-reel tape recorders have become museum pieces, and cassette recorders are similarly becoming superseded technology so that digital recorders are increasingly becoming standard equipment.

Before we even start looking at more specifically linguistic issues relating to the recording of texts, there are some very basic technical issues that you need to sort out first. Before you even go to the field, you need to remember to test your recording equipment to make sure that it actually works. If you are out in the field a long way from anywhere and your recorder won't go, you may have only yourself to blame for the inconvenience.

These days, with the advent of digital recorders, there are often more options on your recorder than you may be used to dealing with on traditional tape recorders. This means that there might be quite different ways of recording, playing, and pausing. Make sure that you become well and truly familiar with the operation of your digital recorder before you go out into the field. People in the field who have agreed to tell a story for you won't be too impressed if you record their well-rehearsed narrative text, only to find that you hadn't correctly put it into 'record' mode. This sounds utterly basic, but even the most experienced of fieldworkers can get things wrong. On my last fieldtrip to Malakula in Vanuatu, I tried to record a story. I had the recorder in readiness in—I thought—'pause' mode, so that I could release the pause button to record the story. When I went to play the story back, I discovered to my dismay that when I thought I was releasing the pause button, I was in fact pausing it, and all I recorded was my storyteller clearing her throat at the beginning and end and I had missed the entire story.

Always keep an eye on your battery levels on your recorder. Losing valuable data because your batteries run out halfway through a story can be extremely frustrating. However, don't assume that it is only your recorder that has batteries that need checking. At the beginning of one of my fieldtrips to Vanuatu recently, I recorded a story which somebody was very keen to tell. When I went to play it back, it started out a little muffled, and it became increasingly inaudible to the point where I could barely make out anything by the end. I tried recording some more material and it was similarly muffled. The playback mode seemed to be functioning fine, and the battery level meter was looking perfectly healthy. I was baffled.

In frustration, I bought a return air ticket to the capital worth about £100, and spent three nights in a hotel—none of which had been budgeted for in my research proposal—so I could go in search of a new tape recorder that worked. In the end, all that I could find that was portable and battery operated was a cheap and nasty little dictaphone with an in-built microphone. I took it back into the field and recorded quite a lot of additional material on the new machine. It worked, though the sound quality was far from brilliant. Since I was recording a moribund language with only about fifteen living speakers, that was a major disappointment.

However, when I eventually returned home and was putting my original equipment back into the cupboard, I noticed a piece of paper that fell out the box that the microphone came in. There was a picture of a little battery inside the handle. It couldn't be so, I thought. But it was. I had been using the microphone for possibly seven or eight years without realizing that the microphone was gradually losing its oomph, and it eventually gave out on me on that trip to Malakula. I didn't need to spend all that money and waste all that time looking for a second-rate tape recorder. I could have fixed my problems with just the cheapest of batteries that I could have bought out in the field.

Given the number of potential disasters that can befall the fieldworker when recording texts, I always like to replay a story in full immediately after I have recorded it. This serves two functions. First, it reassures me that the recording itself is of good enough quality to be transcribed

Secondly, it provides an immediate element of feedback to the person who just told the story. Many people may never have heard their voice on tape before, so immediate playback gives a clear message to the community of what your project is about.

While you don't have to be a studio technician in order to produce valuable recordings in a language, there are some basic points to which you should pay attention. Try to record indoors if you can, to avoid the problem of wind blowing into the microphone. Even a light breeze that you may be totally unaware of can leave you with a muffled recording without your realizing it. Alternatively, you could bring a windshield that slips over the microphone to keep from recording the wind noise. If you are recording indoors, buildings made of traditional materials such as wood, bamboo, and thatch are usually better than buildings with concrete or galvanized iron, because you pick up less echo.

Try to record at a time when there are relatively few people outside. The sound of children playing in the distance is easily picked up on a high-quality microphone, so it is a good idea to record when children are at school if this is possible. I've made the mistake of recording when some-body in an adjacent building was grating yams so the story comes with a constant *kttthhhh kttthhhh kttthhhh kttthhhh* throughout. And you may also need subtly to ask people not to pick nervously at the table or to strum their fingers while they are talking. I once asked somebody else to record a story on my behalf, and the storyteller was scrunching a plastic bag in his hands as he talked. When I went to transcribe the story, it sounded like he was talking through a hailstorm because the microphone was set down very close to where the scrunching was taking place.

I normally introduce any story with a brief comment about who I am talking to, the name of the place that we are in, and the date. This could be in English if you are thinking of some future archivist, but I have generally given the introductions in my Vanuatu recordings in Bislama, the national language, so that my storyteller will feel less uncomfortable with the process. I then indicate to the storyteller that the microphone is his or hers so that the story can begin.

5.1.3 What to record

When you go to record your first stories, you should try to get somebody to tell you a story which is fairly short. Ideally, your first story should also relate to something that you know something about yourself. Perhaps you could ask somebody to tell a story about the day that you first arrived in the field location, or you could ask him/her to give a simple set of instructions about how to light a fire. The first story I ever recorded in Paamese was a set of instructions about how to prepare a yam. It was a very short and particularly unexciting text that went like this:

The yams are dug up. They are brought back. They are grated. They are washed clean. They are thrown into a saucepan on the fire. When they are cooked, the water is poured away. The coconut is grated and it is squeezed. They are eaten.

This text was certainly not a story of earth-shattering importance, but it was just what I needed at that early stage in my fieldwork.

Recording a story about something that you already know something about is going to be helpful to you in the early stages because the more that you and the storyteller share by way of background knowledge, the easier it is going to be for you to understand what the story is about. Your first story is going to be difficult enough to transcribe even in the most favourable of circumstances, so you will want to ensure that there are a minimal number of 'surprises'. When you eventually do get to the stage of recording longer stories about more arcane topics, you will from time to time find yourself confused about who is saying what to whom, or what is the significance of such-and-such an event, and this is a confusion that it would be best to avoid in the initial stages of text recording if you can possibly manage it.

But at the same time, you should reassure your language-helper that they should feel free to say anything at all that they want to say. If they get anxious about 'linguistic purity', you should stress that they should not feel uncomfortable about mixing words from other languages if that comes naturally to them. Usually, the moment people become conscious of any pressure to speak a language in some unnaturally 'pure' form, they become hesitant and lose fluency. Linguists should be in the business of describing, not prescribing, in any case.

You can reassure somebody who feels in any way uncomfortable because they have produced what they feel to be an 'unsatisfactory' story because of the presence of borrowed words by telling them that the story can always be corrected in the written version that you are going to produce afterwards. Of course, if you are going to make this promise to people, you have an ethical obligation to keep that promise. It would be most unfair publicly to distribute a version of a story that the storyteller felt was in some way inadequate where it directly reflected what he or she had actually said.

Once you have become familiar with the basic patterns of the language, and after you have recorded a few texts, you will find that the process of transcription gradually becomes easier and the task will be less time-consuming. At this point, you can start asking for stories about any kind of topic, and stories of any length. You can ask people to tell you stories about anything that they are interested in talking about. People will often concentrate on traditional themes, preferring to tell stories about animals and people in the past that have been passed on from generation to generation.

Stories do not have to relate to traditional themes in order to present linguistically interesting features. I have found that people often have stories about a range of lifetime experiences that they are keen to tell, including stories around any of the following themes:

- the arrival of the first missionaries and the establishment of the Christian church, and conflict between Christian and traditional practices;
- dealings with the first non-missionary Europeans, such as labour recruiters or government agents;
- events associated with the presence of the US military in Vanuatu during the Second World War;
- a major disaster such as an earthquake or a cyclone;
- facing death when lost at sea or when seriously injured somewhere;
- a major trip, such as somebody's first trip overseas.

Sometimes, younger people who have been educated in school may offer to tell a story that hails from another island, or which is clearly some kind of hybrid between a traditional story and an introduced story from outside because of references to non-indigenous animals such as cats.

Once you have made a recording, you need clearly to name the resulting file so that you know what is on it, using a consistent naming convention with no unusual characters. If you are using a tape recorder or minidisc (which I am not advocating!) you should make sure that you identically label both the cover of the tape or minidisc *as well as* the tape itself. You would be surprised how easy it is to label only the covers, only to discover at some later stage that the unlabelled contents are all spread out on the table in front of you and you no longer know what is on any of them!

Since you are going to be interested in any kind of talk, it does not matter in principle what kind of talk it is. Five minutes of gossip and scandalous lies can be just as grammatically and lexically informative as five minutes of a traditional story about the creation of the world. Of course, it would be very unwise to insist on recording anything that you knew to be scandalous and untrue because other people in the community may be outraged by this.

You are probably not likely to face this kind of situation anyway, but something a bit like this may be an issue. When I first started recording stories in Paamese, I would arrive with my tape recorder and ask somebody if he or she would be willing to contribute a story to my collection. Most people expressed interest in the idea but some were reluctant because they said that they didn't know the full story. I remember that my response at the time was something like, 'That doesn't matter, just tell me what you know.' Generally, people were not persuaded by my attempt at reassurance. I can see now that it was proper that they should not have allowed their incomplete knowledge to be recorded because other people hearing or reading their story could easily have criticized them (and me) for getting things only half right. Now, if somebody says that they do not know a story well enough to tell it, I never encourage them to tell half a story. And if somebody says that they need to check the details of a story with somebody else before I record it, I am happy for them to do that.

5.1.4 Reasons for recording

Stories have the potential to provide a variety of different kinds of valuable new information. In particular, stories are used for the following purposes:

(i) *Grammatical expansion.* You cannot expect that elicitation from English will cover all possible grammatical patterns, and it is almost certain that new patterns are going to arise in spontaneous speech. When I had still recorded relatively little textual data on the Naman language of Malakula, I had the impression that serial verb constructions of the type *He cut split the log* were unusually rare in this language in comparison to other languages to which Naman was closely related. However, when I had substantially increased my textual corpus, I came to realize that my initial suspicion was unjustified and that this language had serial verb constructions that are as productive as those of any other nearby language.

Of course, any new constructions which appear in textual data can be supplemented by additional elicitation. Elicited translations from English or some other language may point to the existence of a separate category of past tense on verbs in a language. With careful elicitation, you can complete the full paradigms for the past tense and you may think that you have done all there is to do. However, once you start recording stories, you may find that past tense meanings are occasionally expressed by quite different forms. Further investigation may reveal that the original past tense paradigm that you recorded only related to the immediate past, and there is, in fact, a completely separate paradigm for the distant past. However, your textual attestations of this new paradigm will possibly not provide you with forms for the full paradigm. You would therefore need to supplement the data from your text with further elicited data in order to complete this new paradigm.

(ii) *Discourse patterns.* Many linguists are satisfied simply to produce an account of the phonology, morphology, and syntax of the language. However, it is becoming increasingly important these days also to attempt to describe the discourse patterns of a language, which show how sentences are organized into longer utterances. This is something that cannot be studied simply by taking translations of sentences from English, as it is highly likely that the resulting discourse structures will simply mirror those of English. The only way to get genuine discourse patterns is to get somebody to produce spontaneous speech in the language.

(iii) *Recording oral tradition.* I discussed the need for the fieldworker to provide feedback to the community in Chapter 2. One possible benefit to a community of your research is the recording of oral tradition in written form. As a linguist, you probably would not expect to be able to record a complete set of oral traditions, but there are cases where the recordings of a linguist have become the most important cultural documentation for some people where traditional patterns for the transmission of oral tradition had been completely disrupted.

5.1.5 How large a corpus?

I have referred to the recording of texts in the plural, as it is essential that you record both a substantial amount of material, as well as a varied range of people: young and old, male and female, and perhaps educated and uneducated, urban and rural. It is a good idea to record stories that are both traditional and modern in content so that you can see how new cultural and technological concepts are expressed in spontaneous speech, in contrast, perhaps, to the more prescriptive judgements that you may be offered in direct elicitation sessions.

I have not, however, tried to give any kind of figure for how large a corpus of texts you should aim to produce. For somebody who is working on a moribund language, it may be difficult to obtain more than a few short recordings of continuous speech. My own study of Bandjalang, for example, was based overwhelmingly on elicited data because my language-helper felt she did not have the verbal confidence in the language to provide more than a few short texts.

While even a little bit of textual data is far better than none, the greater your amount of textual data, the more reliable your final grammar is going to be, and your dictionary is also going to be so much the richer as well. Combined with well-directed elicitation, about an hour's worth of spontaneous speech can provide enough information for a moderately detailed grammar. My Erromangan grammar was based on about six hours of speech which amounts to several hundred pages of careful transcriptions. Some linguists, however, have assembled written corpora amounting to several thousand pages of transcribed text. While such large corpora clearly offer wonderful opportunities for the statistical study of variability, I would question the need for such a large corpus if your goal is to produce a dissertation-length account of the grammar of a language.

It is less important to offer any specific guidelines about the size of a corpus than to stress the need to aim for some kind of 'equilibrium' level (Samarin 1967: 68–71). By this, I mean that you should aim to record enough texts that significant new grammatical patterns seldom show up in new texts, and any instances of variability have settled down at reasonably stable proportions with each new text. Once you have reached this stage, you can legitimately shift your attention from the gathering of texts to the detailed analysis of the texts that you have already recorded.

5.1.6 Different genres

I have so far been talking about the recording of just a single style of speaking, i.e. narrative monologues. These are relatively easy for the linguist to transcribe and translate, so they represent a good way to widen your structural and lexical horizons. However, once you have acquired a good selection of narrative texts, you may want to consider widening your horizons by recording other kinds of speech.

You may, for example, want to consider turning your attention to the recording of conversations. Of course, this can be much more difficult to achieve. If you have a group of people speaking together, it is almost inevitable that some people are going to end up speaking at the same time. People are likely to laugh or overlay the speech with other kinds of noise that can at times make transcription extremely difficult. Even when people happen to be taking turns at speaking with clear gaps between each speaker, so much of the meaning in a conversation is taken from the surrounding context that as soon as you have decontextualized the speech in an audio recording, much of what is said may make little sense even to your native-speaker language-helper.

There is also the problem of setting up a workable recording situation for a conversation. For ethical reasons, you cannot record people's conversations when they are not aware that this is being done, so you need to set up your recording equipment in such a way that its presence is obvious, while at the same time not being too obtrusive. You also have to make sure that your equipment is placed in a position where it can clearly capture the contributions of everybody in the conversational group. Finally, of course, there is the problem of how natural people's speech will be in this kind of situation. Arguably, one of the biggest conversation-killers would be the instruction: 'Speak naturally while I record you speaking.'

There are other kinds of situations where it would be legitimate to record people speaking in order to gain access to a wider range of speech styles. You may be able to record sermons or similar kinds of utterances with the permission of the people involved. You may also be able to record meetings while they are taking place. This may involve various kinds of formal speeches which you would not be able to hear when recording ordinary stories. Of course, you may face difficulties in finding a suitable place for your microphone so that you are able successfully to record the contributions of everybody involved. Also, the venue may well be one which does not allow for good quality recordings. You would therefore need to decide how valuable this kind of data would be for your project if you are going to work to overcome the sometimes extensive technical issues involved.

A certain amount of the communicative content of a conversation or people speaking in a meeting is likely to be non-verbal as well as strictly linguistic. In order properly to understand some of what you have recorded, it may be necessary to see some of the various non-verbal cues such as facial expressions, gestures, or body position. Arguably, then, successful conversational analysis or interpersonal exchange can only be carried out by means of video recordings along with audio recordings. While this kind of data can be enormously informative, it clearly requires a lot more specialized recording skills and much more expensive equipment. And, of course, it makes the recording process so much more intrusive.

Further reading: Chelliah (2001), Samarin (1967: 75–84).

5.2 Getting it right

I was somewhat reluctant at first to admit this, but I have not always got things right in my field notes. We linguists like to believe that we are a pretty clever lot and that especially in basic things like phonetic transcription, we are facing a straightforward task. However, I find myself immensely comforted by the following words of Samarin (1967: 22), a field linguist with a considerable amount of experience:

There is probably no linguistic researcher alive, nor will there ever be, who can write down at the first hearing everything which is linguistically significant.

He then kindly goes on to list some of my past errors, as well as the errors about which I have felt so smug when I have discovered them in the work of others:

The errors can be of several types: not hearing enough phonetic differences, hearing differences in the wrong places, wrongly segmenting the stream of sound into phonological units, and so on.

Of course, we have to sort out the inaccurate material from the (hopefully correct) bulk of our notes before we produce our final write-up so that our descriptive account is an accurate reflection of the language as it is used by its speakers.

5.2.1 Evolving analyses

In many cases, somebody who records a little-known language is going to be the only person for a very long time who records anything of that language. I would guess that for a long time, no linguist will want to go and write a new grammar of Paamese in Vanuatu. I would not want to argue that my grammar of the language is perfect or totally complete. However, there are so many other languages that are completely undescribed, that there would not be much point in somebody writing another grammar of Paamese, unless it were to offer a completely different perspective. This means that whatever I have said about Paamese enters the published literature as the only source of information on that language. Of course, if you are working on a moribund language, you may well be the only person *ever* to describe the language in print, as further work may be impossible once the current generation of speakers has gone. This means that you have to be very sure of the accuracy of the information that you present.

As I indicated above, there are some aspects of the grammar of Paamese that I originally published about which I have since changed my mind. I was careful enough to ensure that the actual *facts* that I was dealing with were correct, but there were some points on which my analysis of the facts has since changed. For example, there was a category of what I originally referred to as *verbal adjuncts*, i.e. a kind of adverbial, that I eventually came to realize were a kind of *serial verb* construction. I am talking here about constructions such as the following, in which 'spoke follow' form a serial verb construction:

Na-selūs   usil   meatin   tāi.
I-spoke   follow   person   one
'I spoke about someone.'

5.2.2 Native-speaker error

You must be prepared for the possibility that even a very knowledgeable person with a native-speaker competence in a language can make a mistake while speaking. This means that you cannot automatically assume that because somebody says something, it must be right. People sometimes make slips of the tongue, choosing incorrect words, mispronouncing words, or misusing grammatical constructions for all sorts of reasons. If, when listening to a recording, somebody insists that some kind of linguistic error was made, and you have no evidence that this represents systematic behaviour, then you should not incorporate this into your final description.

I have occasionally been trapped in conversations at parties with non-linguists who, when they have found out what I do for a living, suggest that the kinds of descriptions that I have written are unreliable because of the possibility that I may have been deliberately misled by speakers of these languages. I will ignore the objectionable presuppositions here about there being an honest and reliable 'us' and a dishonest and scheming 'them' and will deal more directly with the question of whether it is possible for somebody deliberately to fool a linguist into producing an inaccurate description.

There are certainly cases where, it is argued, observers have been deliberately fooled into recording questionable data, though this seems to be more likely to affect anthropologists than linguists. Margaret Mead, for example, when she was conducting anthropological fieldwork in Samoa in the 1920s, administered questionnaires to adolescent girls to find out what they were up to sexually. Some of those girls—who are now old women—have recently claimed that they made some information up at that time, partly because they felt that was what Margaret Mead had wanted them to tell her.

In linguistics, it would be possible for somebody deliberately to mislead you in the area of vocabulary. Of course, it would be difficult to imagine what benefit there might be for somebody in doing this, which reduces the likelihood of it happening. One possible scenario, though, might be where particular vocabulary that is associated with secret rites may be withheld from you (Samarin 1967: 28–9). However, it is almost unimaginable that a linguist could be deliberately misled in grammatical matters. To fool even a fairly inexperienced linguist about linguistic structures in a language would be similar to a speaker of English deciding to fool a learner into thinking that the past tense of verbs was marked by the suffix -*ick* rather than -*ed*. Just think how difficult it would be to consistently say *walkick* instead of *walked*. Such a deception would be almost impossible to maintain for any length of time.

While deliberately misleading a linguistic fieldworker is likely to be rare, there are times when speakers unintentionally provide inaccurate information. Some people in a society are likely to be more reliable than others for providing certain kinds of information. Particularly when it comes to lexical information, for example, younger speakers of a language often do not have the same detailed kind of knowledge that older speakers have, so it is best not to rely too much on younger speakers for the collection of information that requires any kind of specialist or traditional knowledge. It is also possible that somebody who is only partly sure about a word's form or meaning may present their information with greater certainty than his or her knowledge warrants, as a way of showing how 'knowledgeable' that person is. For this reason, it is important to cross-check lexical information with other speakers of the language, rather than relying on information from just a single speaker.

Speakers of a language can give you wrong information for other sorts of reasons as well. Your command of the intermediary language may well not be anything like as good as you think it is and it may be that your question was unclear or ambiguous. If, on any occasion, you receive a response which goes against your expectation, you should at least consider the possibility that your interviewing technique may be at fault. It is also possible for a speaker of a language to adjust his or her way of speaking in the direction of yours. If you have not yet mastered the details of the local language—and this is likely to be the case, otherwise, why else would you be there?—then your language-helper may subconsciously be moving in the direction of your own semi-correct grammatical patterns.

In my experience, however, native speakers of languages are much more open about the limitations on their knowledge and they often tell me which information they are sure of and which information I need to check with somebody else with more specialized knowledge. A careful linguist needs to make note of reservations such as this and to do the appropriate cross-checking. It is very easy to forget to add a question mark to a particular lexical entry in your notes and for this form then to make its way into your permanent lexical record. The error in this case would be yours, and not due to your language-helper.

5.2.3 Fieldworker error

A careful fieldworker will not just question the legitimacy of data that comes from his or her language-helpers, but will also be constantly questioning the reliability of his or her own representation of that data, as well as his or her interpretation of what has been recorded. It is not uncommon for one's early data to contain various kinds of errors.

Sometimes data doesn't make much sense because you have broken a single word into two separate words, neither of which makes any sense. Even if you have managed to work out the phoneme inventory, it is often possible to mistranscribe individual words containing sounds that you would never have imagined you would find any difficulty with, and this can also lead you to analyse elements of the grammar incorrectly. The kinds of errors that I have just mentioned are situations where the speaker of the language provides accurate information, but it is not correctly represented or analysed by the linguist.

It is always advisable to write your notes in bound notebooks rather than on individual sheets of paper. Writing on sheets of paper that can be torn out of a writing tablet is not a good idea because once they become detached from the rest of your notes, it can often be difficult to work out if they represent earlier or later notes. You should always clearly indicate at the beginning of each day's writing what the date is, the name of the person whose speech you are writing, and where that person comes from. The advantage of including the date is that it is often helpful to know which form of a transcription represents an earlier—and perhaps less reliable—representation and which is the more reliable later representation. While it may have been perfectly clear at the time that you were writing who you were speaking to and where that person came from, it may well be far less clear who you were talking to and where that person was from when you are back in your office and there is nobody who you can check things with.

It is surprisingly easy for the linguist to get the meaning of a word wrong. This means that a lot of what you record, especially in the early stages, needs to be cross-checked with other people, or with the same person, but much later on in the analysis. One linguist devoted a considerable of effort to recording basic wordlists of about 200 items from nearly 200 different speakers, each coming from a different place. That means the linguist asked the question 'How do you say X in your language?' about 40,000 times. From time to time, the language-helper and the linguist were clearly speaking at cross purposes, and incorrect information ended up being published. On more than one occasion, in response to the question 'What is your word for X?', the person replied with the local equivalent of 'Um...', and the linguist dutifully wrote down the relevant hesitation form as if it were the actual word. This then ended up in the permanent record for those languages.

One common way in which a linguist can make a mistake in the dictionary definition of a word is to assume when somebody gives you an example of what a word can refer to, that this represents the actual meaning. This means that your entry might end up being semantically far too narrow. For example, my early notes on Paamese include the word *romarom* for which I gave the translation equivalent *edible fresh leaf*. Later on in my notes, I recorded the same word, but this time my notes gave two translation equivalents: *tip of something, end of a story*.

When I first recorded this word, somebody must have been explaining to me that the fresh tips of the leaves of a certain plant were edible, and they must have used the word *romarom* to refer to these. I evidently did not realize at the time that *romarom* does not have to refer just to the tips of leaves, as it can refer to the tip of anything at all, and it can even refer to the end of a story. Fortunately, I discovered my initial error before my dictionary was published in this case, but I would have to admit that I cannot guarantee that I have avoided the same kind of problem with every word in every dictionary that I have ever published.

The easiest way for a grammatical error to be incorporated into a final description would be for a linguist to rely too heavily on what may in fact be his or her own clumsy attempts to elicit grammaticality judgements from native speakers. I have already warned about the difficulty of getting reliable judgements from people by simply asking them the question 'Can you say X or not?' It can be very tempting to base a particular piece of linguistic analysis on a single response to a question of this type from a single speaker when other speakers may give rather different sorts of responses. The variability in responses does not necessarily mean that there are distinct varieties involved here. The reality is that grammaticality judgements sometimes need to be expressed as matters of degree rather than as an absolute distinction between grammatical and ungrammatical. Any attempt to treat the data in this way may, therefore, represent an error on the part of the linguist rather than an error on the part of your language-helper.

5.2.4 The problem of tunnel vision

Linguistics is a science, and being a scientist means that we arrive at our conclusions on the basis of empirical observations. Empirical observations, of course, are based on objective reality, without any element of subjective judgement being involved. As scientific linguists, we would like to believe that our field notes are completely free of judgements and that they contain nothing but objective reality. While we may readily jump to the conclusion that some other linguist's notes may be inaccurate, we sometimes seem to be less willing to say the same about our own notes.

On the basis of my own experience, however, I am not sure that we can guarantee that our own notes are invariably perfect. We need to recognize that for at least some of us, our perceptions of what we are hearing may sometimes be influenced by what we were expecting to hear in the first place. The linguistic fieldworker needs to be constantly struggling against the tunnel vision that often comes with whatever happens to be our current hypothesis and which seems to guide our perceptions in the direction of finding further support for that hypothesis, even if it should later turn out to have been wrong.

In the Naman language of Malakula that I am currently working on, there is a phonemically contrastive schwa, along with five peripheral vowels, giving a vowel inventory of /i e a ə o u/. While I have very good reasons for arguing that schwa represents a distinct phoneme in this language, there are some words in which I have found it difficult to decide if a particular vowel is schwa, or if it is instead one of the other vowels. For instance, in the word for 'inside', the phonetic transcriptions in my notes contain both [mbəɣət] and [mbuɣut].

At certain periods during my work on this language, I have leaned towards [ə] being the correct vowel in this word with the forms with [u] representing 'transcription errors', while at other times, I have convinced myself that [u] is correct and that I had been mishearing this vowel as schwas. Depending on which stage of my fieldwork I was at, I rather suspect that I tended to transcribe the word for 'inside' with whichever vowel I was favouring at the time. In saying this, I am effectively admitting that I may not be the world's best phonetician. However, I am prepared to admit this because I am fairly confident that I am probably no worse a phonetician than most other field linguists.

Further reading: Samarin (1967: 148–50).

5.3 Text transcription

The corpus of texts that you have recorded are going to be useful to you only if they have been transcribed. If you are going to produce these in some kind of written form for the benefit of the community, the first step in doing this is also to produce a transcription of the original text.

If battery power for a laptop is not a problem for you in the field, I have found that the easiest way of all to transcribe is to download your audio files from your digital recorder onto the laptop. You will then be able to block the wave form for a section of the text and replay precisely the same stretch of speech as many times as you need. If you are careful enough, you can even zero in on a particular word that you are not sure about and play it as many times as you and your language-helper need in order to decide on the correct transcription. If you are going to transcribe directly from your recording device, then you are going to have to develop a fine touch on the rewind button in order to transcribe material efficiently.

When you first start transcribing recorded texts, the process of transcription will probably be a painfully slow process, for both you and your language-helper, even if the story is fairly simple and short. It is impossible to provide a strict formula for how much transcription time you will need per minute of spoken text, as this will depend on all sorts of considerations such as how familiar you are with the language, how familiar your language-helper is with the process of transcription, how clearly articulated the text is, how good the quality of the recording is, how many disturbances there are while you are transcribing, and so on.

As a rough estimate, however, you can probably expect to spend something like twenty times the length of the original text on your initial rough transcription with the help of a native-speaker language-helper. That is, in order to transcribe a five-minute story, you are going to need to sit down with somebody for nearly two hours of transcription time. I always check a transcription at least once afterwards by myself, which may take that much time again. Any further checks tend to be somewhat quicker, as each additional time that the transcription is checked, the number of potential problem areas is hopefully going to be reduced.

You will need to transcribe exactly what was said on tape, as well as its meaning. You will find that some language-helpers are better at giving you this kind of help than others. Some people, for instance, may want to rephrase what has just been said, on the basis that it was not properly said the first time around. Other people may not want to repeat what was recorded because it contains factual errors of some kind, and they may insist on correcting this. After all, people get details wrong all the time when they are speaking, saying things like 1979 when they mean 1989, saying John when they mean Harry, saying uphill when they mean upriver, and so on. However, you should stress that, while you want to get an accurate record of what appears on tape, you ask people clearly to indicate all corrections which should appear in any version of the story that is going to be made public.

Another problem that you can face when transcribing texts is that some people take what they hear on tape as an invitation to say something else that follows on from this, and it is almost impossible to get them simply to repeat exactly what was actually said. In one language that has only half a dozen elderly speakers left—Ura, spoken in Vanuatu—I once recorded a story from an old lady who is regarded as the best speaker of the language. Unfortunately, when the time came to transcribe and translate her story, she took each section that I played back on the tape as an opportunity to produce yet more language, which I obviously could not record because I was already playing back something else that was recorded on tape.

Sometimes, it can be useful to work with somebody other than the original storyteller to transcribe a story. If the narrator is fairly old and has unclear articulation, you might find it useful to get a younger person to help you with the transcription process. Not only is the younger person likely to have clearer articulation, but you may find it easier to persuade this person not to launch into a related monologue in response to hearing a selection of text.

So far, I have been suggesting that difficulties in transcription can be put down to problems associated with your language-helper, but it is important to realize that you will often be a major part of the problem yourself. I have already indicated that we often develop a kind of analytical tunnel vision that leads us to represent what we hear to some extent in terms of what we *expect* to hear. When transcribing texts, we are quite likely to represent word boundaries, and even the shapes of individual morphemes, according to the particular ways we are analysing the language at the time of transcription.

No matter how careful I think I am being with my transcriptions, from the very first text to the very last, for every language that I have ever studied in the field, I have had to re-transcribe my earliest texts in the light of new analyses that have come to light by the time I got to my later texts. Not infrequently, new material that comes to light in these re-transcribed early texts then leads to new ways of thinking about some of the material in the later texts and those transcriptions then need to be modified. You can probably expect to be transcribing and re-transcribing your texts until you get to the final stages of your linguistic analysis and write-up. Because each of your texts is likely to go through various different forms during your fieldwork, it is always a good idea to date each particular version in case you pick up an old version of a text and you are no longer sure how it fits into your current analysis.

Some linguists prefer to reduce their own role in the process of text transcription by arranging for a language-helper to do this for them. This can be difficult where there is no written tradition in the language in question, as you will either have to teach the person to use (and become confident in) an orthographic system that you may have to devise yourself, or you may even have to teach your language-helper to transcribe texts in the IPA. However, where there is a local tradition of literacy, this can be a good solution. Not only will it free you up to do other things if you have a language-helper produce your transcriptions, but those transcriptions will also be produced by somebody who has native-speaker intuitions about the language.

However, there are possible pitfalls that you would need to watch out for. If there is a local tradition of literacy, this may also be accompanied by a set of somewhat prescriptive attitudes towards the language. If a speaker happens to use a form that differs somewhat from the way that a word is traditionally written, your language-helper may automatically write the word as it is habitually spelt rather than how it was actually pronounced. It will still be necessary, therefore, for the field linguist to cross-check transcriptions.

As a final warning, let me caution against succumbing to any temptation that you may have to take an untranscribed text back home with you with the intention of transcribing it yourself later. Remember, the reason that you have recorded textual data is so that you can encounter new vocabulary and new patterns, so if you do not have access to somebody you can ask about a text, you will not be able to find out what is going on.

I have occasionally tried doing a transcription by myself if my language-helper was not available that day, my intention being that I would be as prepared as I could for when he was available. I would typically find that the first few lines would be no problem at all. There would then perhaps be a single word that I could not clearly make out, or perhaps a word that I had not heard before. That would reduce the amount of sense that I could make of that whole sentence, and if understanding part of the next sentence depended on a good understanding of the previous sentence, I would rapidly get completely lost. Yet the same text, when my language-helper was there to help me the next day, would miraculously become absolutely clear.

5.4 Participant observation

The notion of 'participant observation' is one that is widely used in ethnographic research in the discipline of anthropology. If scholars want to know how people from a particular culture organize their lives and what they believe, there are essentially two contrasting ways of getting access to this information.

5.4.1 Extracting and observing language

One approach to anthropological data-gathering involves the anthropologist living alongside, rather than with, the people they are studying, and asking them a lot of questions. Margaret Mead's work in Samoa was similar to this approach. When she was in Samoa in the 1920s, she lived with an American doctor and she administered questionnaires to people about their behaviour. She was interested particularly in the behaviour of adolescents, and some of her questions involved very intimate details about the sex lives of adolescent girls. In recent years, however, scholars have questioned the validity of some of her central findings, arguing that her methodology was potentially flawed, as people do not necessarily respond honestly to direct questions of this sort, especially on topics such as this one that are regarded as sensitive. I have already mentioned the recent claims of some of the women who were interviewed by Margaret Mead that they used to make up some of the things that they said when they answered her questions.

Participant observation is a contrasting approach to the gathering of anthropological data, which involves living *with* the people who you are studying, and doing the same kinds of things they do, and waiting for things to happen, and simply observing them when they do happen. Somebody wanting to study what people do in Vanuatu when they drink kava, for example, would not do this by asking people questions about what they do when they drink kava. Rather, you would need to go along *with* people when they are drinking kava and observe what happens.

Anthropologists tend to recognize different kinds of participant observation, ranging from *passive participation* to *complete participation*. Passive participation requires you to be physically within the community, but as far as possible to act as a bystander to events so that you can effectively become an overhearer to what happens. This means that in any situation, you need to organize yourself so that you occupy a position physically and socially unobtrusive within a particular context, but which at the same time gives you maximum exposure to the data that you are aiming to record.

It depends on the kind of data you are trying to record how unobtrusive you would need to be. If you are simply trying to find out what the local word for *dog* is, or if you are trying to find out how the paradigm for the present tense of verbs is marked, you clearly won't need to be in a blind spot at all, and you can ask people quite direct questions. But there are certain kinds of observations for which it is much more essential to be unobtrusive. Studying the discourse patterns within interpersonal conversations, for example, would make it much more essential for the fieldworker to be as close to invisible as possible.

Being unobtrusive can mean a number of things. At the simplest level, it can mean being physically as hard to see as possible. If you wanted to record a formal meeting of some kind, it would definitely not be a good idea to be moving around with a hand-held microphone from speaker to speaker. If you are going to be doing this kind of recording, you would need to have microphones set up ahead of time in the right places so that you can be discreetly sitting off to the side somewhere, perhaps monitoring the sound levels on the recorder.

Part of the same requirement is the need to make people from whom you are recording narrative text as comfortable as possible with your recorder. You have to remember that while you are going to be very familiar with your equipment, it may look extremely sophisticated, and even intimidating, to somebody who has not seen it before, particularly if you have a large and bulbous hand-held microphone that you have to thrust in front of somebody's face. I have found myself making a recording in which somebody was audibly nervous, and he was constantly fidgeting with his hands while he was speaking. The resulting story had a far greater proportion of false starts and other dysfluencies than I had found with other speakers of the same language. In retrospect, perhaps I should have allowed the speaker a trial run, perhaps wiping the initial version of the story if the narrator was happier with a second (or third) attempt when he felt more comfortable with the recording situation.

Being unobtrusive may also mean that you should be as quiet as possible. This means that when you are recording talk in a meeting, you should avoid turning the pages of your notebook, or fiddling more than is absolutely necessary with your recorder. This kind of behaviour may effectively bring you out of your carefully chosen unobtrusive position, thereby affecting the data that you are trying to record in some unpredictable way. When I am lecturing to a classroom full of university students, I find that it sometimes takes only a single distraction to throw me off my stride—somebody's mobile phone rings, two people have a whispered exchange—and your fiddling may have a much greater impact on the proceedings that you are recording than you might imagine.

Completely passive participation in a situation is often—perhaps even always—impossible. If you are an outsider, you can never be completely invisible, no matter how much you might convince yourself that you have become truly 'accepted' by members of the community you are working with. No matter how frequently you have used your recorder, it is still something that people can see, and which is different from what happens in their day-to-day lives. Some level of active participation is therefore unavoidable in most cases. Arguably, the more 'foreign' your appearance, behaviour, and language, the more difficult it is going to be for you ever to blend in, so there is a danger that *all* of your observations might be contaminated to some extent by your presence.

What we are really interested in as linguists is empirical data, i.e. data that is based on observed fact. It is axiomatic that there are *no* single-style speakers of any language. This means that everybody's speech is going to vary in at least *some* ways according to the non-linguistic context of the utterance. People will typically use varieties that are considered to be more 'formal' in situations where strangers are present while they will use more 'informal' varieties with family and friends. People are also less likely to use formal varieties when speaking in groups with other people who they are socially close with—this is peer group pressure in action—even if a stranger might happen to be present.

All of these considerations lead us into what is often called the Observer's Paradox. The aim of linguistic research in a community is to find out how people speak when they are not being systematically observed, yet the only way we can obtain that data is by systematically observing them. Very few people can speak 'naturally' when they have been asked to 'speak naturally', especially when there is a microphone and a recorder in front of them, and there is a total stranger from some university sitting there pressing the record button.

The Observer's Paradox comes into play most dramatically in situations where there is a major power asymmetry in the social groupings of the person whose speech is being studied and that of the person conducting the interview. For instance, if one ethnic group in a society is seen historically as being an 'oppressor' and another group as being 'oppressed', the presence of a member of the dominant group interviewing a member of the subordinate group is particularly likely to bring the Observer's Paradox into play.

Many of the conclusions that were reached about the linguistic and cognitive skills of ethnic minority children in the United States in the 1950s, for instance, were based on data that was severely tainted in this way by the effects of the Observer's Paradox. Groups of Black children in the USA were often judged to be linguistically deficient after having had their language skills assessed in formal interview situations with, for the most part, adult White interviewers, who were not previously known to the children. Hardly surprisingly in such situations, children's linguistic responses tended to be as monosyllabic and as non-committal as possible. Such responses then tended to be interpreted as a sign of linguistic deficiency.

William Labov's pioneering work in recording natural speech in the 1960s clearly demonstrated the methodological problems associated with some of these earlier studies. He referred to one record of an interview with a young Black boy in New York City that was used as a basis for conclusions that children like him were linguistically deficient. The boy went into a room where there was a friendly White interviewer. The interviewer showed the boy a fire engine, and then said (Labov 1972: 184–5):

Tell me everything you can about this.

To begin with, the child responded with twelve seconds of silence. The rest of the interview went like this:

Interviewer	*Child*
What would you say it looks like?	8 seconds. *A spaceship.*
Hmmm.	13 seconds. *Like a je-et.* 12 seconds. *Like a plane.* 20 seconds.
What colour is it?	*Orange.* 2 seconds. *An' whi-ite.* 2 seconds. *An' green.* 6 seconds.
An' what could you use it for?	8 seconds. *A je-et.* 6 seconds.
If you had two of them, what would you do with them?	6 seconds. *Give one to somebody.*
Hmmm. Who do you think would like to have it?	10 seconds. *Cla-rence.*
Mm... Where could you think we could get another one of these?	*At the store.*

This interview illustrates the brief and 'linguistically deficient' responses that a lot of investigators had reported in studies of Black children's speech in the United States.

Obviously, though, the child here was faced with an asymmetric testing situation. This child is quite possibly suspicious that if he does or says something wrong, something bad might be going to happen to him. From his experience in school to date, it is quite possible that he had already developed a number of what we might call survival strategies, one of which is to avoid saying anything at all. That is, maybe it is better to say nothing at all than to say the wrong thing.

But different sorts of testing situations with children of the same age, educational level, and socio-economic and ethnic background produced quite different results. Labov organized tests which incorporated the following features:

- The interviewer brought along potato chips, to make the interview more like a party.
- Children were interviewed in the company of one of their friends.
- The interviewer sat on the floor instead of a chair, to reduce the height imbalance.
- The interviewer and the children were matched for ethnicity.
- The interviewer introduced rude words into the discussion.

What these tests showed was that in these kinds of testing situations, children were actively competing to talk. They would interrupt each other, and their contributions were anything but monosyllabic. Here is an extract from one of these interviews (Labov 1972: 188–9):

Interviewer	Children
Is there anybody who says	*Yee-ah!*
your momma drink pee?	*Yup!*
	And your father eat doo-doo
	for breakfas'!
Ooh! [laughs]	*And they say your father - your father*
	eat doo-doo for dinner!
	When they sound on me,
	I say CBM.
What that mean?	*Congo booger-snatch!* [laughs]
	Congo booger-snatcher!
	[laughs]
	And sometimes I'll curse
	with BB.
What that?	*Black boy?*
	Oh that's a MBB.
MBB. What's that?	*'Merican Black Boy.*
Ohh.	

In order to overcome this problem of the Observer's Paradox, we effectively have to divert people's attention away from the fact that they are being formally interviewed. Labov's work in the 1960s demonstrated that these so-called linguistically deficient children, when approached in a testing situation in which they felt less threatened, proved in fact to be highly verbal. It was in his famous article 'The Logic of Non-Standard English' that the Linguistic Deficit Hypothesis was convincingly rebuffed. He was able to do this by reducing the degree of asymmetry between the children and the people doing the testing, and the data that he recorded showed that these children were in fact as verbal as anybody else, though their language did possess certain systematic structural characteristics that other children's English did not possess.

While formal interviews and recording sessions are not necessarily going to produce the most natural patterns of speech, the effect of recording sessions in the kinds of descriptive work that many of us intend to carry out on previously undocumented languages is clearly not going to be the same as we have seen as a result of Labov's work. For one thing, you will almost certainly be recording adults rather than children. For another thing, you are going to be very clearly the learner, and you are not going to be seen as somebody who is administering any kind of a threatening test.

5.4.2 Overhearing in the field

One way of gaining access to natural speech is simply to observe speech that is going on around you. Of course, this is something that you are almost certainly not going to be able to begin with when your own understanding of the language is likely to be minimal. Arguably, in order to be able successfully to 'overhear' a language of which you have no previous knowledge could take many months, possibly even years, of exposure. Let me talk about the kinds of difficulties that you might face.

My data on the Erromangan language of Vanuatu contains both /s/ and /h/, which appear to contrast phonemically, as speakers of the language have provided me with minimal pairs such as *nmas* 'big' and *nmah* 'death'. However, while people claimed that this was a minimal pair, I soon found that in ordinary speech, the word for 'big' is sometimes pronounced as *nmah* rather than *nmas*. While the word for 'death' is always pronounced as *nmah*, when people write the language, they generally—but not always—represent it as *nmas* rather than *nmah*.

This kind of variation between *s* and *h* is widespread in the language, and does not apply just to this pair of words. In fact, almost any word containing either of these sounds can be found alternating with the other sound, though some words seem to be more frequently found with *s*, while other words are more frequently found with *h*. At one stage, I decided to listen carefully for these two alternating pronunciations to see if I could quantify people's preferences. For four days, I noted every instance of the word meaning 'big' that I heard around me to find out how often people said *nmas* and how often they said *nmah*. Although I could have chosen any number of other words, I decided that this was a good word to investigate because it is a high-frequency item. What I found was that 59.7 per cent of the time, people produced *nmah*, while in the remaining 40.3 per cent of the time, they said *nmas*.

Of course, those figures are only as reliable as my ability to recognize instances of this word in daily conversation around me. I had spent many months on Erromango, but my speaking ability in the language was never developed very far. It is a language that exhibits greater morphological complexity than any other language I have ever worked on. I was also only able to spend three months at a time on the island, so although my cumulative period of residence was more than a year in total, every time that I felt I was about to make some kind of conversational breakthrough, I had to leave and start almost from scratch on the next trip. This means that even with the most careful listening for those four days, I may easily have missed a substantial number of instances of people pronouncing either *nmah* or *nmas*.

In principle, of course, if I were ever going fully to document this language, I would need to study the distribution of *s* and *h* in every word in the language. Given that it took me four days of doing nothing else but noting down people's pronunciations of the word for 'big', this would be a huge operation. While frequently attested items such as the word for 'big' would not present such serious difficulties, with infrequently attested items, we face real problems in assembling a representative sample of speech to work out what the appropriate statistical percentages might be.

For example, in Erromangan, I recorded the word *ulehei* 'variety of ginger', which meant that it could be entered into my dictionary files in that shape. I subsequently recorded the word from someone else spoken in a story, where it appeared instead as *ulesei*. In my two instances of this word, I now have a 50/50 distribution between the *s* and *h* pronunciations. Clearly, two instances of a form could hardly be described as a representative sample, so I would need to record the same word from a variety of speakers in such a way that people are not conscious of the kind of linguistic information that I am trying to obtain. If I were simply to wait for people spontaneously to produce this word in ordinary conversation, it could easily take me years before I got enough examples that the figures would be reliable. The alternative might be to test people more directly, but it would be difficult to contrive a natural enough testing situation that would elicit a statistically representative set of occurrences of this word.

Even if I *could* have done this for this particular word, it would not be practical for the remaining hundreds of words that I have recorded with variable *s* and *h* in the language. Given that I was attempting at the time to describe a little-known language for an audience of language typologists and comparative linguists, there were, quite frankly, more interesting things that I would rather have spent my time on. And this is a dilemma that many field linguists may end up facing.

5.4.3 Beyond linguistics

We can't do everything all by ourselves of course, and this is especially the case when we come to recording specialist information, as in plant names and uses, musicology, animals, celestial activity, and so on. Cooperation with specialists in these areas can be extremely productive for all concerned and is to be encouraged, regardless of the pressure from our institutions and funding bodies to work as single researchers.

6
Problems and Pitfalls

I have tried to present linguistic fieldwork so far as something of an exciting challenge. However, it would be unfair to suggest that fieldwork is always going to be easy, and that if you face a particular problem, all you have to do is look up a fieldwork guide for how to solve it. Life is often so much more complicated than that. In this chapter, I want to make you aware of some of the challenges that you may face.

6.1 Analysis in the field

I have deliberately avoided writing this volume as a guide to how to approach the task of carrying out linguistic analysis and of writing up your final grammar, or the compilation of a dictionary. You will find that these can be tasks of enjoyment tempered not infrequently with frustration. However, these kinds of issues lie well and truly outside the scope of this handbook. Linguistic analysis and lexicography are skills that you should have already acquired during your various descriptive linguistics courses before you ever set out on your fieldwork. In any case, there are plenty of well-written volumes already available on the different kinds of linguistic patterns that you can expect to encounter in different kinds of languages, e.g. Shopen (1985a, 1985b, 1985c), Whaley (1997), Payne (1997), as well as manuals for lexicographers, e.g. Landau (1989).

In a guide to linguistic fieldwork such as this, however, it is relevant to talk about some of the issues that relate to carrying out linguistic analysis while you are in the field. While you are doing this, you can expect to face particular problems which are different from the issues that you may have to deal with when you are doing your linguistic analysis back in the comfort of your office at home. You might be tempted to think of your field location simply as a data-gathering site, leaving the entire task of analysis for when you get back home. However, you will need to be doing at least *some* kind of linguistic analysis as you go.

I have already indicated that a field researcher needs to be well prepared for each session of fieldwork with a language-helper. This means that you should come prepared with some kinds of expectations about what you would like to investigate in that particular session. If you are planning on investigating the marking of objects on verbs, for example, you should at the very least come prepared with a list of transitive verbs around which you can construct examples. If you want to investigate certain aspects of the morphophonemics of verbal inflection, you will need to have some kind of preliminary idea about what sorts of allomorphic variants there are in the data that you have already gathered, and what sorts of environments each variant appears in. You therefore need to have checked the behaviour of different types of verbs with a range of different inflectional affixes in order to come to any kind of tentative conclusion that you want to check in an elicitation session.

Linguists seem to vary quite a lot with respect to the amount of further linguistic analysis that they do in the field. I have often envied those who seem to come back from the field with a set of detailed ideas about the structure of the language they are working on. It turns out that many such people were living in a hotel or some other kind of private guesthouse when they were in the field and they then 'commuted' to where they are going to meet their language-helper. People who are working in these kinds of circumstances are likely to have the privacy and working conditions that such conditions entail, and possibly also access to electricity and a good working surface.

In my early work in northern New South Wales, for example, I was able to return after a recording session in the local community to the hotel room that I was staying in nearby. There, I could carefully replay my recordings and come up with tidy final transcriptions before preparing for the next day's elicitation session. The language that I was working on at the time was moribund and I was working with just a single person. Living within the community would, therefore, not have provided me with any exposure to additional data from ordinary spoken conversation, as the language of the community was English. This meant that there was only advantage and no disadvantage to me in living outside the community in terms of carrying out my linguistic analysis. On just one of my fieldtrips to that community, I did make arrangements to stay in the community. While I enjoyed the greater amount of social interaction that I had with people who I was getting to know as friends by that stage, I definitely missed the opportunities to work that my rather more convenient hotel room offered.

In many field sites, comfortable hotel rooms or other private lodgings outside the community are not always available. In any case, there are often very good reasons why it is preferable to live within the community rather than 'alongside' the community when conducting fieldwork. If as a field researcher you find yourself living in the community, you eventually become something like a participant observer, doing many of the same kinds of things that other people do. This means that you will find yourself, depending on your own abilities and interests, helping people to plant their food gardens, bring in the firewood, cook meals, go fishing or hunting, look after children, weave mats, or build a house. If you are doing any of these things with other people, you are going to be in a position to gather much richer and more varied linguistic data. You will therefore be hearing people using the language with each other all the time and in a varied range of situations.

However, the more successfully you make the transition into participant observation while living within the community, the more difficult it is likely to be for you to carry out detailed analysis of your data in the field. One of the reasons for this is that people from different cultures may have quite different sorts of expectations from you about the need for privacy. You may be carrying on your linguistic analysis when you are sitting down by yourself with a pen in your hand, whereas members of the local community may see you as bored or lonely, a problem that can be easily remedied by somebody coming and sitting with you, and perhaps even engaging you in conversation.

Your notion of 'work' and theirs may also be quite different. For local people, work is perhaps more likely to involve sweaty physical travail. While you may think of yourself as 'working' while you are sitting by yourself in order to think about the details of verbal morphophonemics or interrogative constructions, your hosts may well regard your apparent sloth as an invitation to engage in recreational talk.

Even where people do not directly interrupt you while you are working in this way, your activities may attract unwanted attention. On a recent fieldtrip to Vanuatu, I took with me for the first time a laptop computer, which allowed me to download recorded texts. I found it much more convenient to transcribe texts from the laptop, as I could easily block a stretch of text and repeat it as often as I needed. However, many of the people in the village that I was staying in had never had the opportunity to watch somebody working on a computer so I would often end up attracting an audience. People would generally recognize that I was working and they would try to be quiet. But they were watching, incessantly, over my shoulder. And they would occasionally bump the table.

Some people can work when there is a crowd of people watching like this, but it was driving me absolutely nuts. If it's a crowd of children, you can generally solve the table-bumping problem by being a little bit fierce and they will often scatter. But you cannot do that with adults unless you want to alienate people. You simply have to accept that your work is going to be of interest to some people who are passing by. If you find this as distracting as I do, this means that quality time to conduct analysis in the field can be somewhat limited. You may simply have to learn to suffer in silence and continue working. Alternatively, you may be able to turn your disadvantage into an advantage by calling on people in the assembled multitude to help with certain points by asking questions such as 'What was it that he said just there in the recording?', 'What does that word mean?', 'Could you also say such-and-such?', and so on. Alternatively, you may have to be prepared to abandon your plans to work as soon as an audience gathers and do something else.

Fieldwork, therefore, often seems to present us with something of an unfortunate choice between good data access with restricted opportunities for analysis on the one hand, and reduced data access with improved opportunities for analysis on the other.

Further readings: Gil (2001), Rice (2001).

6.2 Learning to speak the language

Probably every fieldworker would love to be able to acquire a good speaking knowledge of the language that they are working on. Some experienced fieldworkers advise that it is *only* through learning to speak a language that you can fully analyse it (Everett 2001). It would be interesting to know how many grammars of languages are written by linguists who do acquire a speaking ability in the language that they are studying. There are some legendary figures in linguistics who have shown enormous flair for learning languages very quickly in the field, including Ken Hale, Kenneth Pike, and Stephen Wurm.

6.2.1 Reasons for trying

There are several reasons why it is a good idea to learn to speak the language that you are working on if you can. First, you will be in a position to broaden your range of structures and vocabulary through exposure to spontaneous conversations that are taking place around you all the time. Secondly, you will be able to engage in monolingual elicitation sessions rather than simply presenting prompts in a lingua franca for translation into the local language. And finally, you stand to have a much more enjoyable time mixing with people. Through local people's appreciation of your knowledge of their language, you will no doubt improve your own motivation.

One does not need to be able to speak a language in order to analyse it. I indicate in the preface to this volume that I have published accounts—or am currently working on accounts—of as many as eighteen different languages, though I never tried to carry out even a basic conversation in most of these. Many of the descriptions that I have produced involve moribund languages, so I faced few natural opportunities for conversation in the language in any case.

However, while I was working on my doctoral dissertation on Paamese, I found that after about six months on the island I was increasingly able to live monolingually in Paamese, and by the time that I left after twelve months, I was resorting very little to Bislama, the local lingua franca. I figured that I had made a real advance when I fell asleep while some people were playing cards nearby. I woke up because I was feeling cold and my card-playing friends poked fun at me because they said I had been talking in my sleep. (I learned a new expression that day: *selūs ramobong* 'talk in one's sleep'.)

Since I had never known myself to be a sleep-talker, I asked, 'What did I say?' They replied, *An gat vāreinaus*. This literally means something like 'Cold is just a lot biting me', which is a normal way of saying in Paamese 'I am really cold'. I asked, 'What language did I say it in?' They replied, 'You were speaking in Paamese'. That surprised me, but what surprised me most was the form of my message, so I asked, 'Did I say *An gat vāreinaus* (a construction which I didn't actually know about yet) or *An gatinau vārei?*'. This is a simpler and more English-like construction that I already knew about, which literally means 'Cold is biting me a lot.' They confirmed that I had used the construction that was not consciously familiar to me, but which I had presumably internalized from conversations that I had heard around me, but had not yet dealt with in my direct elicitation sessions.

6.2.2 Reasons for success or failure

The authors of most published grammars, however, are surprisingly reticent about their own conversational abilities in the language in question. Perhaps this is because they are being modest, but my suspicion is that many are somewhat reluctant to let it be known too publicly that they did not manage to become very conversational in the language. I have certainly not been able to match my own success in learning Paamese in some of the other field situations that I have been involved in. While I was working on the island of Erromango, for example, I did get to the stage where I could say things to people in the local language, but any kind of extended spontaneous verbal exchange was beyond me.

I suspect that there are several reasons for my relative success in learning Paamese and my relative lack of success in learning the language of Erromango, and these factors may be relevant for other field linguists as well. First, having published a grammar of both languages, I would argue that the Paamese language exhibits fewer structural complexities than Erromangan. Of all of the languages that I have ever described, Erromangan is the most complex, with verbs especially exhibiting considerable morphotactic complexity, as well as involving a substantial amount of morphophonemic variation in the shapes of many of the affixes, including a fair amount of unpredictability and irregularity.

The relative ease of Paamese and the relative complexity of Erromangan is matched by the vastly differing extents to which outsiders have acquired a speaking knowledge of the two languages. There are many non-Paamese from other parts of Vanuatu who have learned to speak Paamese, while there are very, very few non-Erromangans who have ever learned to speak Erromangan.

Second, the size of the Paamese-speaking community in comparison to the Erromangan-speaking community may be a factor. There are probably more than three times as many speakers of Paamese as of Erromangan. Large numbers of speakers of Paamese also live in the capital, while there are relatively few Erromangans living in town. This meant that whenever I went to town, I was able by and large to continue to live in a Paamese-speaking milieu, while this would be almost impossible in the case of Erromangan. Paamese households in town would often be exclusively Paamese-speaking, but households involving Erromangans would very often be linguistically mixed, resulting in much greater use of Bislama, the lingua franca.

Third, I have detected something of a difference in outlook between Paamese and Erromangans in regard to their languages. While both groups of people are proud of their languages, the Paamese almost seem to be aggressively proud of theirs. I never had to ask people on Paama to dispense with Bislama and to speak to me in Paamese. They initiated the switch themselves. They would constantly say things to me in Paamese. Only if I didn't understand would they then repeat it in Bislama. Eventually, when I understood enough in Paamese and even began replying in Paamese, people simply refused to speak to me in Bislama. The Erromangans, however, never demonstrated any similar kind of linguistic chauvinism.

But my success in learning Paamese and my failure with Erromangan was not due just to these three factors. The way in which my time in the field was organized was also a factor. While I spent a total of just over twelve months living on both Paama and Erromango, my fieldtrips to Paama involved two visits of six months' duration, while my time on Erromango involved four visits of three months each. It wasn't until I had spent six months on Paama that I felt confident enough to carry out spontaneous conversations in the language. By the end of my shorter stays on Erromango, I would typically feel that I was about to make a breakthrough in terms of my speaking ability, but then I would leave. When I came back, I would find that I was more or less back to square one.

Different individuals are presumably going to have different kinds of language learning abilities and are going to require, therefore, different periods of exposure before they can become conversational. For me, it seems that six months of continuous exposure was enough to acquire a knowledge of Paamese. Samarin (1967: 54) seems to think that this period should be enough for most, though I have been envious of others in the past who have managed this after three months, and I have found myself feeling smug about other people's linguistic inabilities after twelve months. The only way you are going to know what your own abilities are is to go to the field and find out.

The factors that I have just discussed are unlikely to be the only factors that are involved in acquiring a speaking knowledge of the language of your field site. Another possibility to consider is the extent of the role that the local lingua franca already plays within the linguistic repertoire of the local community. If the lingua franca is well established as a part of the local linguistic scene for certain communal functions, then it may be more difficult for members of that community to wean themselves off a reliance on the lingua franca in their dealings with you.

One of the reasons that I chose to work on Paama in the first place was the fact that this was a relatively small island on which no other language was spoken. My rationale was that the Paamese people would be unlikely to use Bislama with each other, except perhaps when an outsider was around. My prediction turned out to be correct, and when I was on Paama, the only outsider was in fact myself. This meant that I was exposed to almost nothing but Paamese from the outset.

Before I had decided on Paama, I originally considered a number of other field sites. I gave some thought at one stage to working on Malakula. I decided against this because there are at least two dozen actively spoken languages on this island, as well as another dozen or so languages that are now moribund. I guessed that with such diversity on the island, Bislama would play a much greater role within the various local communities. I am now involved in a long-term project on Malakula and can confirm that this is very much the case.

I have spent a total of about twelve months living in the village of Vinmavis. While the primary language of this village is very clearly Neve'ei, Bislama also has an important role. Because this language is spoken in just a single village with a population of about 500, many men have married women from other language groups. In some cases, these women have learned to speak Neve'ei, but many of the younger wives use Bislama with their husbands and their children. Because these women become fully integrated into the community, on most communal occasions, Bislama has become the dominant language. Thus, community meetings and church services are almost invariably conducted in Vinmavis in Bislama rather than the local language. One of the church congregations in Vinmavis has also recently set up a private school which caters to children from a wide area of northern Malakula. Students who attend this school all board with local families, but because these children all speak different local languages, Bislama also comes to be a household language even where the husband and the wife both come from Vinmavis and speak Neve'ei.

6.2.3 Individual differences

Some people are likely to be more successful than others, partly because of the circumstances in which you find yourself, and partly because of different individual aptitudes. You will therefore need to become comfortable with whatever level of success you can achieve. However, you almost certainly would not need to become a proficient conversationalist in the language in order to impress people in the local community. For many small local languages, few outsiders will ever have acquired a speaking ability in the language, so people will not necessarily expect you to manage this anyway. You can possibly expect great tolerance of your efforts to speak the language as long as it is clear that you are trying.

Although there is no single formula by which anybody can successfully learn a language, there are some tricks to help make thing easier. If you have an affinity with young children, they can often be your best informal language teachers. Young children are more likely to be monolingual, so they will not find it strange to speak to you in their language, and they will not have acquired the kinds of social graces that prevent them from correcting you when you have made a mistake. I remember once walking barefoot through a Paamese village with a young boy and I hurt myself when a sharp stone poked into the underside of my foot. I cried out in pain and the boy asked me in Paamese what had happened. I responded, *Ahat tā dilīn hēk* 'A stone poked my foot'. My young interlocutor perfectly straightforwardly said that the proper way to say this was *Ahat tā sal hēk*, which literally means 'A stone speared my foot.' I went *Ah* to indicate that I had got his point. However, this was not enough for him and the little boy said, 'OK, say it then.' So he forced me to repeat the sentence with the correct choice of verb. I have never forgotten that lesson.

Adolescents and adults, by way of contrast, may have quite different attitudes to the use of the local language. They will typically have learned a lingua franca and may be reluctant to use the local language with you, finding it easier to stick with using the lingua franca. Somebody who has been to school may also want to interact with you in English in order to practise their English, while you are looking for people with whom you can practise your knowledge of the local language. An adult speaker of Paamese would probably have simply accepted what I said when the stone hurt my foot. This is because my meaning was no doubt obvious, in spite of the apparently odd way in which I framed it.

I have already referred to my lack of conversational confidence in Erromangan. During some of my time on the island, there was an American Peace Corps volunteer working in the same village that I was staying in. I had heard her speaking Bislama, in which she demonstrated adequate proficiency, though I would not have described it as a sophisticated command of the language. However, when I visited other villages, people would speak in raptures about this woman's ability to speak the local language. I was struggling quite badly with the language at the time and I have to admit that I was rather envious. I felt this particularly strongly since I was there to do nothing but language work, while the Peace Corps volunteer was sitting down with somebody for a few hours at weekends when she was not otherwise fully occupied with teaching in school.

My envy, it turned out, was somewhat misdirected. The American approached me at one stage for help in language matters and it became apparent that she had not even been able to work out how some of the most basic of noun phrase structures worked. It was clear that she had made little progress in working out the grammar, and she could not possibly have been genuinely 'speaking' the language. But she had certainly done the right thing in learning the main greetings and linguistic formulae and she used these regularly. Not only this, but she had also learned a small number of basic vocabulary items. Her ability to say just *good morning* and *goodbye*, while also knowing that a *nup* was a yam, impressed local people hugely.

Conversational fluency might be too high a goal to set for many people, while an ability just to express greetings is surely too low a goal. Most people should probably aim for something between these two extremes. Unfortunately, there is no magic bullet when it comes to actually acquiring a speaking knowledge of any language and this is something that can only come with hard work and with constant practice. In the case of a previously undescribed language, you will obviously not be able to buy a set of tapes and language lessons before you go to the field and you will just have to learn on the job as best you can. You are simply going to have to get used to asking people how to say things.

You will then have to try using the patterns that you have uncovered with other people. Of course, you may have to develop a thick skin, as you are almost certainly going to make mistakes, and sometimes people are likely to find at least some of your mistakes uproariously funny. One of the reasons that young children typically make much better language learners than adults is that children have fewer inhibitions, and they are more willing to learn from their own mistakes. An extroverted adult is therefore likely to make a better language learner than an introvert. If you are more introverted, you can of course still succeed at language learning, but it will possibly take you longer to realize that you can get your message across if you force yourself to give it a go.

However, I have already indicated that local people will often be remarkably generous in their judgement of your linguistic abilities. I don't know how often I have heard Paamese people say that I speak Paamese 'better than the Paamese'. This is absolute nonsense, of course, but this story seems to have started some years ago when I was able to show people that I had learned to count up to twenty (and beyond) in Paamese. Since most younger speakers of the language can only count up to five in the local language and beyond that they use numerals from the lingua franca, Bislama, my counting ability seemed impressive. In reality, my conversational abilities in Paamese were probably never worth much more than a B+, but a little reverence of this kind can certainly spur you on.

Further reading: Samarin (1967: 50–5).

6.3 Going troppo

I have talked about a wide range of issues and problems relating to the conduct of fieldwork. Fieldwork is almost certainly going to be a major learning experience for you as a fieldworker. Much of the impact of fieldwork on the individual is positive, in that you gain exposure to a new culture, to a new language, and to new friends. At the same time, however, you cannot expect everything about fieldwork to be positive.

Before my first fieldtrip to Paama in 1976, I was already experienced enough in the practical side of fieldwork from my previous work on Australian languages that I did not anticipate any major problems adapting to my new situation. Admittedly, I was going to have to learn a new language in order to carry out my fieldwork. However, before arriving on Paama, I spent about a month in Vila doing some basic lexical and structural elicitation with Paamese speakers there, and I had even recorded some short texts in the language which I had transcribed. I used this month to acquire a basic conversational competence in Bislama. By the time that I arrived on Paama I felt that I was 'set to go', and I was really looking forward to the experience.

I fairly quickly found a place to stay, and found that people in the village that I had settled in were very friendly and welcoming, inviting me to all social functions that they themselves attended. I did not aim to do any serious linguistics for a while, as I thought it would be useful to get the 'lie of the land' before I tried to do too much. Once I decided that I was ready, I started recording linguistic data, and things were progressing well. I worked this way for about three months, and was making satisfactory progress.

After about three months, however, things began to change. I began to feel that my work wasn't progressing as quickly as it should. I began to get a little worried because I had a doctorate hanging over my head that depended on my gathering a healthy amount of data. My arrival on Paama had unwittingly ended up coinciding with the time of the annual yam-planting season. Clearing the bush, preparing the ground, planting the yams, and tending the growing vines is heavy work that the entire community has to be involved in. It simply wasn't 'on' for me to expect people to absent themselves from their community responsibilities to sit down and work with me on linguistic matters. As the yam-planting season progressed, I was getting increasingly anxious that my own linguistic work was suffering.

Given that everybody was away from the village working most days, I simply tagged along with the work parties. I even joined in the work where there were things that I could do. I was able to gather some yam-planting terminology in this way, though the amount of data that I was recording for the physical effort that I was putting in was fairly small. I continued to worry, though I was at the same time having a wonderful time mixing with people and learning new things.

However, the anxiety that I was feeling about my linguistic project and the social mixing that I was doing were beginning to feed on each other. After about three months of being constantly in the company of a village full of people, my slight worry was starting to turn to stress. I had up till then been used to living by myself while I was a university student in Australia. When I came to Paama, however, I found that I was unable to take off by myself whenever the fancy took me. I could not go for a walk by myself in the bush. If anybody saw me heading off by myself, at least one other person would feel obliged to tag along. It turned out that there was a reason for this: if I went by myself, I would be subject to all manner of supernatural forces in the bush that I was not equipped to handle. I might, for example, accidentally walk through a taboo place, which, it was believed, could place either my life or health in danger, or the life or health of other people. In the view of the Paamese, it seemed that I needed constant baby-sitting.

My inability to spend time by myself, coupled with a growing anxiety about the lack of progress in my work, led me to go troppo. This is a somewhat traumatizing experience in which you crave for familiar experiences, and you begin to resent the unfamiliar. This leads to occasional hostility towards people who feel they have acted in a completely friendly and supportive manner towards you. A touch of paranoia seems to be part of the collection of symptoms, and it is far from pleasant.

Nobody had told me to expect this to happen before I went to Paama. Once you begin to experience culture shock, possibly the best way to overcome it is to have a short break away from the field location and come back refreshed. Eventually, my rather negative feelings passed and I got used to my situation. In fact, once you overcome this fairly uncomfortable period, your time in the field can become immensely enjoyable, and you may eventually experience great sadness upon leaving.

Different people may experience difficulties with different aspects of a particular culture. In most parts of Vanuatu, people have converted to Christianity in the last century or so and people today are generally devout Christians. People in most communities attend church regularly. The Sabbath is fairly strictly observed in many places, with no manual work being permitted, and there are sometimes even limitations on doing anything that could be construed as having fun, such as frolicking in the sea. The idea that one might be an agnostic or an atheist is difficult for many people to understand, so some attendance in church by a visiting linguist is possibly a good idea. Many westerners do not say grace before meals, but people's religious traditions in Vanuatu generally call for somebody to say grace before the meal is started. The visiting linguist may even be called upon to contribute from time to time, so it is worth being prepared.

Whether one is a man or a woman can also influence one's reaction to particular elements of the local culture. In many traditional rural societies, men have rather more freedom than women, and this may also include visiting linguists. Women may also be expected to exercise modesty in dress and behaviour that may seem restrictive at home. In Vanuatu, for example, while men are free to smoke and drink alcohol, women are not. Women are also not expected to wear slacks, and they certainly do not wear shorts and T-shirts. Visiting western women may to some extent be granted 'honorary male' status in that some aspects of non-standard behaviour may be tolerated, but it is always necessary to be fairly subtle when testing what may be acceptable and what may not.

You can also expect that sexual mores will be quite different from what you are used to at home. Of course, local people will have their own preconceptions of the sexual mores of westerners, who may be perceived as not being subject to any kind of restraints. What may to you be a completely innocent happening, such as a conversation between a single female fieldworker and a young unmarried local man, may have quite a different meaning altogether. I remember once having a perfectly innocent conversation in broad daylight with a female visitor to Erromango from New Zealand and behind her back, but in my line of sight, the local young men were giving me all sorts of encouragement with their winks and smirks. For these kinds of reasons, it is often best for female fieldworkers to work with female language-helpers, and for male fieldworkers to work with male language-helpers, unless there is a substantial age difference between the two.

Not everybody goes troppo. Those who do experience it find that it comes in differing degrees, and that it manifests itself in different ways. In my case, there was some depression, as well as irritability towards particular people (especially those who had become my friends, and who were therefore with me most often). There are probably just as many solutions to culture shock as there are manifestations of the phenomenon in the first place.

6.4 Getting caught up

I discussed participant observation as a way of gaining access to linguistically valid data. I did not mention at that point that you can expect participant observation to lead to a variety of different kinds of social relationships within the community. Some of these relationships can be immensely rewarding, while others end up being more like entanglements than rewarding relationships.

6.4.1 Becoming part of the scene

If somebody is more than just a short-term visitor, it often becomes necessary for them to be incorporated in some way into the local community structure. In some cases, you may well end up being 'adopted' by a particular family, thereby acquiring a mother and a father, brothers and sisters, and nephews and nieces. While this kind of welcome can be flattering, it must be remembered that children in paid employment may have extensive obligations to support their rural parents and siblings financially, and this privilege may end up being extended in your direction as well.

While this could be viewed as an inevitable fieldwork expense, it is something that you may find it difficult to justify to your university's accountants. You may therefore be forced to do a little creative accounting by which that pair of running shoes or that watch that somebody persuaded you to buy mysteriously appears as an amount of money under some other budget heading.

Alternatively, you may end up having to fork out from your own pocket, though this will depend on how deep your pocket is. Trying to explain to somebody that you simply cannot afford some particular item may not be easy. People may find your protestations of poverty, even if you are a graduate student, difficult to believe, because you are still likely to be much better off than local people in many parts of the world. I have been quizzed in the field about my income, and people have only wanted to know my total income. They have not been the slightest bit interested in hearing about the rather smaller amount left after national and local government taxes, mortgage payments, insurance, deductions for health care, compulsory union fees, savings for retirement, and utilities.

You may occasionally also be questioned about the possibility that you are going to make lots of money selling books about the language that you are working on. While some linguistic descriptions have no doubt earned good money for both the authors and the publishers, none of the linguistic descriptions that I have produced fall into this category. Relatively few people are aware that most academics earn little or no direct income from royalties, so you may have to explain something about the economics of publishing to members of the local community. (Of course, there is a sense in which we do gain less directly from the products of our research, in that we can go for a promotion, or seek a more prestigious or a better-paid job at another university on the basis of our publication record.)

6.4.2 Unexpected entanglements

There is a host of additional kinds of involvements that you may end up being caught up in, sometimes completely unintentionally, and the ultimate outcome of these involvements may be much more difficult to predict. I once did some very brief grammatical elicitation on the Neve'ei language of Malakula with a speaker of the language who was studying in New Zealand. I subsequently accepted an invitation to spend Christmas with his family on Malakula to see in the year 2000. This was an invitation that I was keen to accept, as I decided that I would prefer to say farewell to the 1900s well away from the hoopla that seemed to be enveloping the rest of the world over the advent of the new millennium. A small remote village with no electricity, hence no TV, seemed like an excellent option to me.

Shortly before I left for Malakula, I discovered a number of previously completely unanalysed texts in Neve'ei that were recorded by the British anthropologist Bernard Deacon when he visited the area in 1926. That was at a time when people were still living a largely traditional lifestyle up in the interior of the island. While his material was sufficiently well transcribed to allow it to be recognized as Neve'ei, it needed some careful checking by a linguist to correct some of the phonetic transcriptions.

On the day after Christmas when people in the village were relaxing, I took out my photocopied pages of Deacon's stories and explained that I had found some stories in their language in an old book which I now wanted to write out correctly. Since Neve'ei is not a written language,

I expected that people would find it difficult to recognize words from the written page, particularly as a number of unfamiliar phonetic symbols were used. I therefore adopted the strategy of attempting to read what Deacon had written and I then asked people either to indicate if what I had said was correct, or, if it was not correct, I would ask them to say what it should have been.

When I had finished going through each story word by word, I then read it back in its entirety to check that I had it right. The first time I did this, the reaction from my audience—which had grown quite substantially out of curiosity from the single individual who I had initially approached—was one of considerable amusement, not to mention amazement. After all, here was this *khabat* 'European' who, after having been in the village for a mere three days, seemed to be able to speak the local language.

Word rapidly seemed to spread about this unusual *khabat*, and people began dropping around with requests for me to 'tell a story in the language'. Although I said I couldn't 'tell a story' in the language, people were happy enough for me to read one, especially since practically nobody in the village had ever had an opportunity to read their language themselves. This quickly developed into something of a party trick that I would be asked to perform, and these story-readings became sources of amusement and amazement for people of all ages. While some of the stories that I was 'telling' were well known, one was of particular interest, as most people had never heard it. However, one old man informed people that he had in fact heard the story himself when he was a boy and that it was correct in all of its details.

By this stage, I must admit that I was enjoying the attention somewhat, as it is often difficult for someone from another culture, especially on a short visit to a place such as this, to find something that one is sufficiently good at that one can make a serious contribution. Some people were apparently giving more serious thought to the significance of my party trick than I was. My host's father volunteered the information that I was not the only person in history with this particular ability. Long ago, he said, there had been another *khabat* who surprised people by turning up with the same ability. The Neve'ei-speaking people have only been Christians since the 1940s. Prior to this, people occupied a series of bush hamlets, practising their traditional culture in the interior adjacent to the coastal area where they now live. At that time, a *khabat* visitor arrived speaking the language, and also participated in their traditional dances and took part in the grade-taking ceremonies that Malakula is famous for in the anthropological literature.

I was told that he was an Englishman by the name of *Teken*. This was very obviously Deacon's name in a Neve'ei form, which had been enshrined in oral tradition since 1926. Although Deacon was welcomed initially, things at some stage apparently went wrong. I was told the story of how he took it upon himself to visit a place called Lebelang up in the interior where he should not have gone. This place is still regarded today as being very powerful, and the consequences of trespass in the pre-Christian 1920s were severe: the old people resolved that Teken should be killed and eaten. However, he was spared, possibly because people would have been aware of likely serious consequences from the colonial authorities of such an act against a British citizen.

Deacon left the area for the southern part of Malakula, where he had already carried out a considerable amount of more detailed ethnographic work. According to the story as it was told to me, when he got back to southern Malakula, he fell ill and died shortly afterwards, in 1927 (see Gardiner 1984: 75). When a young and otherwise healthy person dies on Malakula, this is frequently attributed to a variety of mysterious and malevolent forces. It is easy to imagine that people at the time would have seen Deacon's death as some kind of natural consequence of his transgression against their taboos.

I was told that the tradition was for people to be buried with their heads to the setting sun. The people at Southwest Bay, however, were reported as having buried his body with his feet facing in the direction of the setting sun, with the intention that this would make him 'come back'. Presumably, those responsible for this interpretation of the manner and the significance of his burial had a better impression of Teken than the old people from the Neve'ei-speaking area who had wanted to kill and eat him, and who probably saw in his death some kind of appropriate retribution.

Meanwhile, back in Vinmavis in 1999, when Christmas was over and before the new year, this was interpreted in Vanuatu—as just about everywhere—as representing the end of the old millennium. This came to be associated by some people with potentially earth-shattering events. On two occasions, I remember being asked at the time by local people whether I thought that the world would end at midnight on 31 December.

There was also an almost comical rush of weddings in the capital, as people who had been living together for years in unsanctified 'bush marriages' were keen to have church marriages performed, apparently so that they could non-adulterously face their maker on New Year's Day.

People in Vinmavis seemed to me to be approaching the new millennium much more rationally. The local Presbyterian church building was showing very visible signs of having endured many years of cyclones, earthquakes, and the normal wear and tear that buildings are subject to in a coastal environment in the tropics. It was decided that the last communal act of the old millennium would be for the entire congregation to come together to demolish the old church building. The date set aside for this was 28 December 1999. People would then rebuild their church from new foundations at the beginning of the next millennium.

The task of disassembling the church was completed with great speed and efficiency, leaving just a crumbling concrete foundation after two or three hours of sweaty and dusty work. However, a few hours before the final service to deconsecrate the old church was due to begin, I was approached by a member of the church committee and asked if I would agree to participate in the programme by telling one of the stories that Teken had written down. My initial response was to say that I would feel very uncomfortable about the idea of standing up in front of the entire village and being presumptuous enough to dare to tell *them* one of *their* traditional stories in *their* language, and probably not very well at that.

The church committee member persisted and he was clearly not going to take no for an answer. It quickly became apparent that there was more at stake here than just my own sensitivities. This was being seen as a historical occasion at the turn of the millennium. My coming to visit so many years after Deacon was buried with his feet to the setting sun, and having an ability to tell the stories that he had recorded, was surely too much of a historical coincidence for such a contribution to be missed. I therefore acceded to the request, though not without considerable trepidation on my part.

The story that I chose was the one which I already knew to be no longer widely known, but whose accuracy had already been confirmed by the older people. I will not say much about the story itself, other than to comment that it related to some particularly un-Presbyterian subject matter involving corpses, cannibalism, and defecation. I judged that my telling of the story went surprisingly well despite my own extreme nervousness and the apologies that I expressed beforehand in case I spoke unintelligibly, made mistakes, or mentioned subject matter that some people may have objected to. Whatever shortcomings there were in my delivery, I clearly spoke intelligibly enough because it was a story that I am certain was intended to provoke laughter, and the congregation laughed in all the right places. When I finished, I scurried back to my pew to a round of spontaneous applause, feeling relieved that the experience was over, but gratified and humbled by the response.

I have already indicated that the word that the people of Vinmavis use to refer to Europeans is *khabat*. According to the traditional belief system, the same word is also used to refer to a ghost-like individual with superhuman powers who is of great cultural significance. *Khabat* were also supposed to be able to be reborn as children after their death. These *khabat* are supposed to have been able to perform various kinds of magic, and also to have had white skin. It is not too surprising to find that the first Europeans to visit Malakula also came to be referred to as *khabat*. Not only do Europeans qualify in terms of physical appearance, but their technology, even in the nineteenth century, could easily have appeared magical. For instance, they had long sticks which could be pointed at a pig or a person and which would make a loud noise. The pig or person would then suddenly fall over dead without anybody's direct touch. This long stick—a rifle—came to be called a *nivis khabat*, because it could be used to do the same thing as the traditional *nivis* 'bow', but in a much more mysterious and dramatic way.

Although Malakulans today still refer to Europeans as *khabat*, I am quite certain that people do not regard Europeans as ghosts. Europeans are not assumed to have superhuman powers, and everybody now knows that the secret of the rifle is that you go to the store and buy bullets. Judging by the way that the people in Vinmavis who I got to know were interacting with me, I never felt as if I was being treated as anything but fully human. Whenever small children burst into tears of fear at the sight of me, this was not because they are told that white people are ghostly bogey men, but because they are doctors who give them much-dreaded injections.

Some may be tempted to argue that the use of the word *khabat* to refer both to powerful ghostly beings and to Europeans is an indication that Malakulans think that Europeans are really returned ghostly ancestors of some kind. There are certainly plenty of examples of reports from elsewhere in the Pacific of Europeans at first contact—and even of linguists and anthropologists well after first contact—being said to be 'ghosts'. However, when I have carried out fieldwork in Vanuatu, or when I have simply been visiting people socially in rural areas, I had never been faced with any kind of situation where there could have been even the remotest possibility of this kind of interpretation, so I tended to be a little sceptical of claims of this kind, suspecting that people were perhaps overinterpreting—or even misreporting—their experiences.

Deacon's appearance in 1926 would have been early enough that in many parts of Malakula he would probably have been the first European that some people had ever seen. He may therefore even have been assumed by people to have been a *khabat* in the traditional non-human sense, rather than in the modern human sense, and he hinted at this himself in a letter from the field to a correspondent in the UK: 'Here come the men and I must talk to them about offerings to ghosts. I am a ghost' (Gardiner 1984: 45). If a signal was sent to the people of Malakula that Deacon was planning on returning after his death by being buried with his feet facing in a particular direction, this may well have sat comfortably with the belief system of people at the time.

This all leads to some fairly heavy questioning of the role of the ethnographer and of the linguist in the community which he or she is investigating. Many traditional anthropological and linguistic descriptions make practically no reference at all to the investigator or to local people's reactions to him or her. However, all observations in which an observer is present are based on what happens while he or she is engaged in observing people, and it is the outsider who is then interpreting that behaviour for the reading audience. It is because of this that I feel that I could not ask people in Vinmavis the very question that anthropologists would probably most like an answer to: Am I Teken returned? If so, in what sense might this be the case?

For some people, it would surely be a ludicrous question to ask, as well as pretentious and/or insulting. Such a question arguably operates on the presupposition that Third World people who are frequently represented as ethnographic subjects might be somehow less rational than westerners, as has been argued by Obeyesekere (1992). Yet, for other people, this may not be such an impossible idea to suggest, though it would have to be recognized that there are different levels at which people could hold such beliefs. Some people may take the literal view that if Deacon was to be regarded as a *khabat* in the traditional sense (as well as in the modern sense), then any suggestion of a later reincarnation is tantamount to blasphemy and to be rejected outright by any modern Christian. On the other hand, other people may view any possible 'return' of Teken more metaphorically, with my appearance in Vinmavis being Deacon-like in certain unexpected respects at the turn of the millennium. Finally, of course, there is the possibility that the interpretation may be taken literally.

I suspect that it would not be possible to offer any single interpretation of the events which I observed—and in which I unintentionally ended up participating—in Vinmavis over the Christmas/New Year period of 1999–2000. My presence, as well as my ability to tell a long-forgotten story in the local language, was obviously a fortunate coincidence which allowed me unwittingly to become part of the millennial symbolism in Vinmavis, rather than the simple bystander as I had originally anticipated. Because of the role that was thrust upon me, however, it is difficult for me to seek the precise meaning that my presence had at that historic moment.

Further reading: Kulick (1995: 268) (Appendix: On being a ghost).

6.5 Linguists behaving badly

Successful field research depends on an ability to maintain good relations both with the individuals with whom you are working and with the community at large. In some cases, relationships may become strained and this can even threaten the viability of a project. In extreme cases, similar kinds of projects which might be proposed for some time in the future may even be jeopardized. Sometimes, an individual may be personally responsible for having the welcome mat withdrawn, while in other cases, things may go wrong for reasons that are well outside your own control.

At the level of interpersonal relations, people from different cultures can generally find ways of getting on together in spite of their differences. It may be something of a cliché, but all it takes is a little sensitivity and a willingness to learn. Obviously, I could not hope to offer practical lessons in how to behave in a culturally appropriate way in every cultural group, so you will need to discover for yourself what the local faux pas might be so that you can avoid them.

But it is not difficult to make a mistake, in which case you need to hope that people in the local community are going to be tolerant of your weaknesses. For instance, when carrying out fieldwork in Vanuatu, it is most unwise for a visiting linguist to drink a fair amount of wine and to follow this up with the consumption of a fair amount of strong kava. (The wine, of course, facilitated the misjudgement in the first place.) The result of this kind of behaviour is that a certain amount of cleaning up becomes necessary, and one's sense of dignity can take something of a beating. However, the visiting linguist may also be called in the next day for a more formal talking-to from the local chiefs, which will require a certain amount of humility, along with a formal apology.

Of course, sometimes, people do the wrong thing as a result of their own straightforward stupidity or even deliberate pig-headedness. So serious may the blunder be that one researcher may sour a community's attitude towards more thoughtful researchers in the future. I remember hearing of one linguist who decided to jump into a community's supply of drinking water to have a wash. Not only was that linguist not invited back, but I could well imagine that local people would have been somewhat wary of inviting any other linguists into the community for some time to come.

If your fieldwork is being conducted from the vantage point of a temporary resident of a local community—arguably, I have repeatedly suggested, the best way of obtaining the richest and most reliable data—you also need to remember that you are somebody's guest. You will of course have included some provision in your fieldwork funding to compensate your hosts in some culturally appropriate way. As a thoughtful guest, you should also be prepared to muck in and help with household tasks. If you end up in a working party of people digging a hole for a new toilet or bringing in next week's supply of firewood, you should be prepared to treat this as a new experience, as well as an opportunity to hear the language being used in new contexts.

Having no doubt hosted visitors of your own in the past, you will also be aware that sometimes guests can outstay their welcome. You need to bear in mind that while people may genuinely be pleased to host an overseas visitor such as yourself, your presence may sometimes also represent something of a burden. Before I started fieldwork on the island of Erromango in Vanuatu, I visited a friend there socially for a week while I was on holiday. As soon as I arrived, my friend's mother said something to him in a low voice which, it turned out, was an anxious question, 'What am I going to cook for him?' I quickly assured his mother that she didn't have to put herself out at all. I would be happy, I said, to eat anything at all that the family was eating. My only special requirement was a cup of tea first thing in the morning, and I made sure that I brought my own packet of tea with me that I could share with the family.

Local people typically get their first cup of tea when the women of the household have finished cooking the bananas, and this tends to be around 8.00 a.m. Unfortunately, by then I would be getting the first pangs of a caffeine-withdrawal headache, as I am very much a morning person, and first thing for me is around 7.00 a.m. (at the very latest). To cater for my needs, my host's mother could be heard chopping the firewood to get my cup of tea ready shortly after birdsong in the early morning while I was still lying in bed.

While I was perfectly capable of lighting a fire and boiling the tea myself, I realized that it would probably be a major task for me every morning to get things organized. As I was a visitor, I wouldn't necessarily know where the axe was that morning to chop the firewood, where the matches were to light the fire, where the kettle was, where the cups were, and so on. Since I was intending to be there for just a week, I thought it would probably be best just to accept my host's mother's generous accession to my special caffeine-related need. When I returned on my next visit, this time with the intention of staying for three months of fieldwork, this kind lady immediately reverted to her early morning tea preparation mode, just for my benefit, and once it had started, it became extraordinarily difficult to do anything about it.

This is just a small example of how easy it is for your presence to affect a local family's routine. I am hoping that this particular burden that I had accidentally imposed was not too onerous, as the fire would have to be lit every morning, whether I was there or not. However, there are times when the burden could become a problem. I am currently working in a village on Malakula in Vanuatu. The area where this village is located is prone to extended dry periods. While water is piped into the village from a distant spring, a land dispute was causing somebody to interrupt the flow of water from time to time in order to make a point.

At one point, for a whole week, we were having to bathe either in the sea, or in slightly smelly (and certainly not drinkable) well water. I began to think that if this water problem persisted, the whole community would begin to face serious problems with drinking water. I decided that if things got much worse, I would have to consider leaving. While my departure would certainly not solve the drinking water problem, it would at least have saved people from having to worry about me in addition to their own problems.

People in the past have sometimes appropriated valued cultural artefacts and taken them away in violation of local custom or wishes. In many countries, laws have been passed to prevent this kind of behaviour, but this has not stopped 'art collectors' from stealing artefacts in violation of national laws. Although field linguists typically do not get involved in such activities, there has sometimes been a residue of suspicion that attaches to us, because local people do not always find it easy to distinguish between a linguist, an anthropologist, a legitimate art dealer, and an art thief. In some cases, the climate of suspicion has been strong enough for all social science—including linguistics—to be banned for extended periods.

Some linguistic fieldworkers become so obsessed with the need to become participant observers that, at some level at least, they try to convince people that they have crossed the boundary between 'us' and 'them'. Of course, it takes far more than an ability to speak the local language, much more than a willingness to go around barefoot, and more than a penchant for wearing some form of traditional dress or adornment to change one's ethnicity. While it is perfectly possible for a linguist to adopt local traditions as a way of being respectful, and local people may even encourage you to do this, nobody will be fooled into believing that you have become one of 'them', even if you might believe this yourself.

One linguist has reportedly been correcting local people for years when they are speaking their own language. He appears to have no idea how insulting educated members of this language community find this kind of behaviour. I know of another field linguist who made a point of using one of the local languages in a formal meeting with government officers where all of the local people were using the official languages of the country. Although the linguist presumably wanted to make the point that the local languages should be treated as being important, nobody at the meeting understood the content of his talk. The experience was apparently quite embarrassing for all concerned, apart from the linguist who was oblivious to the reaction.

Sometimes, the insensitive behaviour of field linguists extends also to their own colleagues. There was a linguistics conference that was held at the University of Papua New Guinea about twenty-five years ago in which most of the papers were presented by people who were doing fieldwork on some of the many different languages in the country. Presenters and discussants in the various sessions—who were almost exclusively non-Papua New Guineans—were repeatedly saying things like 'in my language, we say X' and 'in my village, people say Y'. This use of phrases such as 'my language' and 'my village' can be taken as an arrogant usurpation of somebody else's language and identity by English-speaking academic linguists from overseas, or as a thoroughly naive and precious attempt to demonstrate to other linguists how successfully he or she has been able to 'go native'.

Further reading: Vaux and Cooper (1999: 10–21).

7

Salvage Fieldwork

The term 'salvage' fieldwork refers to the study of languages that are moribund, i.e. the language is being documented because it is realized that it is rapidly disappearing. This kind of fieldwork often involves particular problems that go beyond any of the topics that I have discussed already in this volume.

7.1 Getting started

This subheading is the same as the title of an entire chapter which appeared earlier in this volume. While some of the issues relating to salvage linguistics are the same as those that we encounter when working with communities where vibrant languages continue to be spoken, there is a whole raft of additional issues which relate specifically to the commencement of salvage fieldwork that must be discussed separately.

7.1.1 Responding to the enthusiastic

Finding linguists who are willing to conduct this kind of fieldwork is one issue. A lot of descriptive grammars these days are written by graduate students carrying out research for the doctoral dissertations. Some linguists may write only a single grammar, one which is written for their doctorate. When prospective graduate students are looking for languages to describe, the preference is overwhelmingly to work on languages which are still being actively spoken within vibrant speech communities rather than on languages with just a handful of remaining speakers.

I was recently approached by a member of the Orkon community, which originally occupied part of the west coast of the island of Ambrym in Vanuatu. This language is now moribund, with fewer than twenty speakers living in two different villages where another language has become the primary medium of exchange. On the basis of my ongoing research involvement in Vanuatu, I also regularly receive requests from intending graduate students from a number of different universities around the world for advice about suitable language communities in which to carry out doctoral research. I would love nothing more than to meet requests from these graduate researchers with this direct request from a speaker of Orkon by advising somebody that they should carry out research on this language, which very clearly does not have a healthy future.

However, I do not feel that I could do this. A grammar that is detailed enough to meet the requirements of a doctoral dissertation needs to be based on information that can only come from exposure to a language that is still actively spoken by an entire community. While some of the remaining speakers of Orkon no doubt still have an excellent command of the language, it would be almost impossible to observe the language being used to any great extent in a natural way. All speakers of Orkon almost certainly spend most of their time speaking other languages rather than Orkon. It seems to me that it would be unfair to send a graduate student to record data under these kinds of circumstances when so much depends on their ability successfully to complete their doctorate.

Ideally, this kind of situation calls for an experienced field linguist who already has a doctoral degree and for whom it is not nearly as important to be able to produce a detailed and comprehensive grammatical description. In this case, there are several linguists who could be called upon to help, including myself. However, established linguists are also quite likely to have extensive teaching commitments during term time, as well as longer-term research commitments that are already under way, which can make responding to such a request difficult. The end result is that languages that are in greatest need of documentation are sometimes those which are least likely to be described.

What is particularly gratifying in the case of Orkon is that there is a member of this community who is keen to see the language documented. We can only hope that this enthusiasm succeeds in bringing a linguist on board to carry out the kind of salvage fieldwork that is so clearly needed. My own work on the moribund Nāti language of Malakula (Crowley 1998a) came about as a result of a similar burst of local enthusiasm.

At the end of a short social visit to Malakula, when I became stranded with the closure of the airstrip due to heavy rain, one of the last speakers of this language recognized an advantage to him in my misfortune and took me to the local store to buy some exercise books and pens, found somewhere quiet where we could work together without interruption, and proceeded to get me to write down as much of his language as I could in the few days that I had available before the airstrip was reopened. Interestingly, when one of this man's relatives saw us working together on his language, he was asked how much *he* was paying *me* to record all of his linguistic data, which indicates how valuable a task this was seen as being. (Needless to say, I did not accept any money for the task that I had performed.)

7.1.2 Persuading the reluctant

However, despite the obvious value of the documentation of moribund languages in situations such as these, it is sometimes surprising for linguists to find that proposals to carry out this kind of salvage work may be met with varying degrees of interest from the communities involved (Gerdts 1998). My own experiences of fieldwork on moribund Australian languages in the 1970s involved acceptance of my activities at best, with some outright hostility, but never, as I cast my mind back, completely enthusiastic support. Aboriginal people in the areas where I worked had suffered major demographic decimation, communal degrad- ation, and personal exploitation and humiliation as a result of many decades of social policies and communal attitudes that were paternalistic at best, and downright destructive at worst. This led to strong feelings of linguistic and cultural loss. All of this made it very easy for people to regard any unfamiliar European linguistic fieldworker either as yet another intrusive and exploitative agent of government, or as yet another patronizing and interfering (or even racist) member of the community at large.

Under these conditions, salvage fieldwork was far from easy, and a field linguist had to acquire a thick skin quickly. One reputedly good speaker of the then poorly documented Gumbaynggir language in northern New South Wales, for example, simply turned her back on me when I said that I was not in a position to pay her thousands of dollars for the privilege of recording her language. Of course, I did have some funds at my disposal with which to pay those who made their time available to work with me, though the amounts were far more modest than what was expected on this occasion. While other people did not demand large sums of money, they certainly did not always go out of their way to make themselves easily available to work with me.

I encountered other less negative reactions as well, and many people did allow me to take up their time to record what they knew of their ancestral languages, even if that was sometimes only very little. However, my memories from the 1970s are by and large of having constantly to encourage—and sometimes even cajole—people to continue to participate in this process of linguistic documentation in order to meet the expectations of academic linguists. Those were the days before this kind of research was governed by Ethics Committees which require participation to be uncoerced. The advice that I was given at the time, when faced with these kinds of situations, was to appeal to people's sense of guilt by saying 'I have a bossy professor who will not allow me to come back empty-handed'. I cannot remember now if I ever made use of that specific piece of advice, but it is advice that should never be given to a field linguist today.

While we often assume that people all over the world are proud of their language and the distinct identity that the language expresses, the reality is sometimes a little more complex. Some people view a knowledge of the local language as a sign of unsophistication and ignorance, and find it embarrassing that a foreigner might want to study it, and this can make it difficult for a project of salvage fieldwork to get off the ground. Lyle Campbell (pers. comm.) reports that it is quite common right across Mexico and Central America for indigenous people of many different groups to have been made ashamed of their local language by the Spanish-speaking majority and many conceal a knowledge of the language because of this.

Many try very hard not to be identified as Indians, particularly when away from their communities. People often talk about *Indios revestidos* 're-dressed Indians', where *Indio* is extremely pejorative, as bad as—or worse than—the N-word in English. The image expressed in this phrase is that members of indigenous groups will dress in western clothing to try to look un-Indian and thus not suffer the slurs and prejudice. If outsiders come to a village and ask someone if they speak the local language, the answer will commonly be 'no' even when they do. This is partly because of the sense of shame that being 'Indian' brings, and partly from a distrust of outsiders who have a history of coming in and cheating native peoples out of their land and deceiving them in many other ways.

7.2 Working with a limited number of speakers

One of the major problems that we face when carrying out salvage linguistic fieldwork is the very small number of people who speak the language. In extreme cases, there may be just a single remaining speaker of a language. Quite a number of linguistic descriptions in Australia have been written on the basis of information drawn exclusively, or almost exclusively, from a single speaker. In fact, my own published salvage studies of Yaygir, Bandjalang, and Mpakwithi in Australia arose out of material that was gathered in this way from single speakers of each language.

7.2.1 Diminishing speaker populations

Earlier in this volume, I pointed to the danger of attempting to write an account of a living language on the basis of a single speaker who has been dislocated from his or her language community. Whatever limitations there are on the validity of a grammar which has been written without access to observations of spontaneous usage would presumably be equally applicable to salvage fieldwork that has been carried out under these circumstances. This means that my own accounts of Yaygir, Bandjalang, and Mpakwithi quite possibly misrepresented the true nature of the language in certain respects. The problem is that we will now never know the extent to which this is true, and what sorts of defects there may have been in my accounts of those languages, because in each case, the final speaker who I worked with in the 1970s has since died.

Of course, a language can have more than just a single speaker and still be moribund. It is probably more likely that there will be at least several people who can speak a language, or maybe as many as ten or twenty. Whatever the precise number of speakers, when you are attempting to describe a moribund language, the small size of the remaining population of speakers means that you are often not going to be able to choose your language-helpers in the same way that you can when you are working in a vibrant language community. This means that you will simply have to make the best use of whoever is available (and willing) to work with you.

Because of the age of speakers, it is quite possible that somebody's physical frailty may be a real factor in limiting their ability to work with you. I know of one linguist who had been invited by somebody's family to record something of one language but it turned out that their elderly relative was so frail that he could not get up from his bed. In this case, the only decent response was to explain to the family that this kind of work would be an intolerable burden on the old man and to promise to come back when he was feeling better. In the end, that was not possible and the old man died, but at least he was able to spend his final months with his family rather than with an intrusive linguist.

In other cases, people may have put you in contact with somebody who may be physically quite strong but who may be suffering from some kind of dementia. This can make it difficult to elicit meaningful and reliable responses to questions, so opportunities for grammatical and lexical work may be limited. On one occasion, I was asked to record a story from one old man and he produced a long account of a historically significant event that he remembered from his youth. However, when I played the story back to other people who could understand the same language, they threw up their hands in despair. They basically declared the story to be untranscribable because the old man was rambling, sometimes incoherently. To this day, that story has not been transcribed.

In some cases, you may find that you have to deal with an elderly person's insufficiently clear articulation. I have already indicated that an older person may fail to grasp the notion of the paradigm, thereby preventing you from acquiring a full range of allomorphic variation. This may not be a problem with a language that has speakers spanning all generations, as you can probably expect to find somebody else who can help you with this kind of elicitation.

Further reading: Evans (2001).

7.2.2 Diminishing structures

When a language has become moribund, it will not only become restricted to a small group of relatively elderly people, it will also become restricted in the range of contexts in which it is used. Sometimes, the remaining speakers will end up living in quite different locations, in which case the language may be used on only those very rare occasions when the remaining speakers get together in a single location. Even then, the opportunity to use the language may be very limited, as the language that has become the dominant language of the community is likely to intrude. With few opportunities to use the moribund language, it is only natural that people's command of the language will begin to suffer.

There have been a number of studies of the effects that this kind of functional and demographic restriction can have on the lexicon, the phonology, and the grammar of a language. It is very likely that a speaker of a moribund language will exhibit all kinds of unsystematic variation between the moribund language and whatever happens to be the dominant language of the community, and possibly also in the direction of the language of elicitation.

When I was working on Bandjalang in the 1970s, for example, I found it difficult to elicit spontaneous textual data, so my description was based for the most part on data translated from English prompts. It turned out that the word order in the Bandjalang data that I collected as a result was predominantly SVO, just like my English prompts. This, however, is somewhat suspicious, given that Australian languages tend either to have SOV word order, or they have completely free word order. There are other facts about Bandjalang which make it look as if the speaker who I was recording data from was being influenced in her word order by the sentences that I was giving her in English.

There are other situations involving moribund languages where a speaker is clearly mixing in vocabulary items, and even grammatical constructions, that belong to the major actively spoken language in the area. There are only about half a dozen speakers of the Ura language of Vanuatu, all of whom also speak the Sye language. Whenever I tried to record Ura data, there was always a component of the data that looked suspiciously like Sye rather than Ura, and it became necessary to 'weed' this data out. It also turned out that some individuals were more likely to produce 'contaminated' data than others, so it was necessary to work out who were the more reliable speakers, and who were not, and to take everybody's data into account when producing the final description. The grammar of Ura that I eventually produced was therefore not simply an analysis of my corpus, as I had to weed out certain data first that I had deemed to be 'contamination' from the other language.

When a language becomes functionally and demographically restricted in these sorts of ways, sometimes the last speakers no longer have anything like a full command of the language. Such speakers are often referred to in salvage linguistic studies as partial speakers. Situations can vary quite considerably as to how impaired any individual's capability in a language might be.

It is quite possible that somebody may not realize until you come along and start eliciting lexical and grammatical data that they do not know nearly as much of the language as they—or other people in the community—thought they did. It could be quite harmful for a linguist to come along and effectively show a respected elderly member of the community up as somebody who knows very little. You must remember that one of the overriding ethical obligations of the researcher is to bring about no harm to your research subjects.

It is essential, therefore, to be constantly on guard when working with partial speakers for possible limits to their knowledge. You can expect that in the vocabulary, less common and more specific kinds of terms are less likely to be remembered than more common words. If you ask for the words for highly prominent body parts such as head, nose, eye, and mouth, you stand a good chance of getting a positive response. However, you should avoid asking for words for fontanelle or molar teeth in your first elicitation session because people can sometimes feel embarrassed if they are repeatedly made to demonstrate a lack of knowledge.

It is more difficult to predict what sorts of limits there may be on people's grammatical knowledge, but the same kind of problem can arise. When I was working with one of the last speakers of Bandjalang in northern New South Wales, it became apparent that nouns could be marked for plural, but that the precise morphological means by which this was achieved varied according to the semantic type of the noun. Thus, nouns referring to trees tended to behave one way, while nouns referring to birds tended to behave in another way, and so on. It also became apparent that there were quite a lot of exceptions to any of these generalizations, so it was important for me to test every single noun to obtain its plural form. It soon became apparent that I was not going to be able to obtain a plural form for every noun. My language-helper answered confidently when she was able to, but at other times looked somewhat awkward. Eventually, she said 'Oh, the old people never told me about that sort of thing', which I took as a signal that I had possibly already probed too far for her comfort.

It is important, therefore, for the fieldworker always to show gratitude for and interest in the data that you have been able to record, and never to show any kind of disappointment if you have not been able to record as much as you thought you would be able to. I remember speaking to an old man in the 1970s who, I had been told, was the last person who knew anything of the Nganyaywana language of northern New South Wales. This was a language that linguists were particularly interested in at the time, as Nganyaywana was thought to be a linguistic isolate, i.e. it was completely unrelated to all of the other Australian languages. When I spoke to the old man, he was only able to remember the name of the language and one or two other words. A decade or so before another linguist had recorded quite a number of additional words. By the time I came along, however, his memory had clearly faded and this was disappointing. However, it was important to express gratitude for the knowledge that he had been able to share.

While I have heard many stories of linguists having arrived too late to be able to record information that an elderly last speaker once knew, things do not necessarily always work out as badly as this. Evans (2001: 262–3) reports on several different situations involving work on moribund languages in Australia where speakers' knowledge of the language showed signs of improving as elicitation with a linguist progressed. Thus, what originally may look like an unpromising situation may turn out to offer rather more to a patient linguist.

7.3 Legitimate linguistic authority

When a language can claim only a handful of elderly speakers, you might assume that all of these speakers will exhibit the same kind of interest in seeing their speech recorded as a basis for your description, and that all speakers can be equally expected to be able to provide information. Perhaps a little surprisingly, this is not always the case.

I am currently working towards the documentation of the Tape language of Malakula in Vanuatu. This is a language which currently has between ten and fifteen speakers, with the most confident speakers now in their seventies and eighties. People in this community are very keen for this language to be documented, and my activities as a linguist are being strongly supported. People have arranged for me to record a number of texts from the older members of the community. I found the task of transcription and further elicitation arising out of these texts quite difficult because the old man who was regarded as the best speaker articulates his speech in a way that I find quite difficult to hear. He is also somewhat hard of hearing, which means that I have to speak quite loudly in order to be heard. Finally, he finds any of my attempts at paradigmatic elicitation quite frustrating, as he feels that I am simply asking the same word over and over again. I began to despair at one point of ever succeeding in producing a description of the language.

It turned out that the son of the old man, who is now in his fifties, is also a speaker of the language. He is married to somebody who speaks a different language and nobody in his household speaks even a single word of Tape. He considers his own knowledge of Tape to be inferior to his father's knowledge, as his father spent his childhood living in an entirely Tape-speaking community in their original homeland. His father was part of a migration out of that homeland more than fifty years ago into the area where members of this community currently live amongst speakers of a quite different language.

When I found out that the old man's son could speak the language, I asked if he would be willing to help me to transcribe his father's stories. He agreed, but when I arrived at his house at the appointed hour to start work, he was nowhere to be found. I eventually found out that he felt that his command of the language would be inadequate to the task and that he was really unwilling to offer his services because he saw his father as representing the 'true' language. His disappearance to go to his food-garden was an excuse to avoid disappointing me.

When I explained to him later that all I wanted him to do was help me to write his father's words, he agreed to give it a try. It turned out that his knowledge of the language was more than adequate to the task and we completed the task together without difficulty. Understanding this man's sensitivities, I somewhat gingerly approached the possibility of him recording a story for me in Tape as well. Now that he realized that his knowledge was not nearly as inadequate as he had originally thought, he agreed to give this a try. Eventually, he volunteered several stories, and then sought out other speakers younger than his father who he thought could record in the language as well.

There is a second reason why people may express reluctance to be recorded which relates not to their perceived inadequate command of the language, but to their lack of a legitimate genealogical connection to members of the moribund speech community. There is another old man who speaks Tape. He originates from another language community but as a young man, he spent a lot of time with speakers of Tape and learned their language. The result is that he is now one of that very small number of elderly people who can still confidently carry out a conversation and tell a story in the language.

However, while people from the Tape community have made various arrangements for me to record stories from a number of different people, that old man has never figured in those arrangements, nor has he himself made any request to me to be allowed to tell a story. I once hinted at the possibility that he be asked to tell a story, but I quickly found people changing the topic of conversation, seemingly to avoid following up my suggestion.

I suspect that I will never have the opportunity to record his speech because, although he speaks Tape as well as anybody else, he is not of Tape ancestry himself. A significant motivation for community members in supporting my project to document the Tape language appears to involve the role that the language plays in demonstrating a connection with ancestral Tape lands. Because this Tape speaker does not play a legitimate part in that task, his knowledge of the language appears to be of little interest to direct descendants of the original speakers of Tape.

7.4 Saving the language?

There can be something of a problem involving salvage fieldwork relating to the expectations of the community. In a salvage situation, people often interpret your interest in documenting the language as an implicit promise to 'revive' the language. While in practical terms all you can do is document the language for future generations, a different understanding of your intentions (and capabilities) can sometimes develop within the local community. If you were to fail to deliver on what might have been seen as some kind of a promise, this has the potential to result in disappointment, and even anger.

I sometimes find myself dismayed when I encounter stories in the mass media which claim that some overinflated linguist who claims to be an international expert on language preservation is about to embark on a project to 'save' some particular dying language, when in fact all that person is going to do is document the language. It is more than unhelpful when such linguists claim to be doing precisely what we are not in a position to do; it is, in fact, unethical.

Any responsible linguist needs to make it absolutely clear to members of the local community what their intentions are. They have an ethical obligation to explain to members of the threatened language community that while salvage descriptions may be of considerable historical interest to members of the local community, as well as being of interest to historical linguists and linguistic typologists, we are in no real sense 'saving' the language.

This kind of linguistic documentation does nothing more than conserve data in a language purely for the historical record, effectively 'museumizing' the language. Obviously, museums have their importance in terms of documenting earlier cultural practices and in conserving the artefacts associated with those cultures. However, there is no sense in which such institutions 'preserve' cultures or languages as living systems. While nobody would seriously propose bulldozing Stonehenge because it derives from a culture that is no longer practised, very few people would seriously argue (one hopes) that recording something of a dying language is a completely pointless exercise. Such historical information is important for local community members, for linguists, and also for humanity in general—but we must not allow ourselves to be misled into believing that we are in any way 'saving' the language. Saving a language is a much more complex and much more demanding task than this.

Some members of the Erromangan community of Vanuatu responded to the appearance of my description of the moribund Ura language of their island (Crowley 1999) as allowing for its revival as a spoken language. However, it is practically impossible to imagine any scenario by which this could realistically be expected to be achieved. It is unimaginable that people on the island could successfully teach themselves the language from my book, or indeed from any book, given the levels of functional literacy in the community. Apart from the fact that the account of the language itself is less than comprehensive, language learning obviously requires a considerable amount of direct contact with a speaker (or, ideally, many speakers) of a language.

The most confident speaker of Ura is now very old and physically frail, so any attempt at instituting something like an immersion programme for young children would be impossibly demanding on this person. Material resources on the island are extremely limited and the kinds of well-trained and committed people who would be needed to run relevant community education projects are extremely thin on the ground. This has meant that even vocationally oriented programmes that might be seen as giving people access to means of earning money such as carpentry and dress-making have often proved difficult to set up and maintain. It is difficult, therefore, to see how people on this island might be able successfully to implement a language revival programme, especially in the absence of any kind of local linguistic expertise, along with the absence of any institutional back-up for such a programme in the local linguistic ecology.

Of course, the kinds of materials that you end up producing may be taken up by members of the local community for some kind of language programme. My publications relating to some of the languages that I documented in the 1970s from northern New South Wales and far north Queensland have since been incorporated into locally run language programmes geared towards members of the local communities. It is unlikely that these languages will ever again be used in spontaneous conversation, but the languages do have an important symbolic function for these communities as expressions of local identity. A knowledge of these languages also signifies a historical link to the past, and in Australian law, this kind of link can be a significant fact in demonstrating a legal right to owning areas of land.

Further reading: Himmelmann (1998).

References

AUSTIN, PETER. 2006. 'Data and language documentation'. In Jost Gippert, Nikolaus P. Himmelmann, and Ulrike Mosel (eds.), *Essentials of Language Documentation*, 87–112. Berlin: Mouton De Gruyter.

—— and TERRY CROWLEY. 1995. 'Interpreting old spelling'. In N. Thieberger (ed.), *Paper and Talk: A Manual for Reconstituting Materials in Australian Indigenous Languages from Historical Sources*, 53–101. Canberra: Aboriginal Studies Press.

BARLEY, NIGEL. 1983. *The Innocent Anthropologist: Notes from a Mud Hut*. Harmondsworth: Penguin Books Ltd.

BOAS, FRANZ. 1911. 'Introduction'. In *Handbook of American Indian Languages*. Bureau of American Ethnology, Bulletin 40, i. 1–83. Washington, DC: Government Printing Office (Smithsonian Institute).

BOUQUIAUX, LUC, and JACQUELINE M. C. THOMAS. 1992. *Studying and Describing Unwritten Languages*. Dallas: Summer Institute of Linguistics.

BRADLEY, DAVID. 1998. 'Minority language policy and endangered languages in China and Southeast Asia'. In Kazuto Matsumura (ed.), *Studies in Endangered Languages*, 49–83. International Clearing House for Endangered Languages Linguistic Studies, 1. Tokyo: Hituzi Syobo.

BRADSHAW, JOEL. 1994. Review of *A Dictionary of Paamese. Oceanic Linguistics* 33(1): 257–62.

CHELLIAH, SHOBHANA L. 2001. 'The role of text collection and elicitation in linguistic fieldwork'. In Paul Newman and Martha Ratliff (eds.), *Linguistic Fieldwork*, 152–65. Cambridge: Cambridge University Press.

COMRIE, BERNARD. 1981. *Language Universals and Linguistic Typology*, 2nd edn. Chicago: The University of Chicago Press.

CROWLEY, TERRY. 1978. *The Middle Clarence Dialects of Bandjalang*. Canberra: Australian Institute of Aboriginal Studies.

—— 1979. 'Yaygir'. In R. M. W. Dixon and Barry J. Blake (eds.), *Handbook of Australian Languages*, i. 363–84. Canberra: The Australian National University Press.

—— 1981. 'The Mpakwithi dialect of Anguthimri'. In R. M. W. Dixon and Barry J. Blake (eds.), *Handbook of Australian Languages*, ii. 146–94. Canberra: The Australian National University Press.

—— 1982. *The Paamese Language of Vanuatu*. Canberra: Pacific Linguistics.

—— 1983. 'Uradhi'. In R. M. W. Dixon and Barry J. Blake (eds.), *Handbook of Australian Languages*, iii. 306–428. Canberra: The Australian National University Press.

—— 1992. *A Dictionary of Paamese*. Canberra: Pacific Linguistics.

CROWLEY, TERRY. 1993. 'Tasmanian Aboriginal language: old and new identities'. In Michael Walsh and Colin Yallop (eds.), *Language and Culture in Aboriginal Australia*, 51–71. Canberra: Aboriginal Studies Press.

—— 1995. *A New Bislama Dictionary*. Suva: Institute of Pacific Studies and Pacific Languages Unit (University of the South Pacific).

—— 1998. 'A salvage sketch of Nāti (Southwest Malakula, Vanuatu)'. In Darrell Tryon (ed.), *Papers in Austronesian Linguistics No.5*, 101–48. Canberra: Pacific Linguistics.

—— 1998. *An Erromangan (Sye) Grammar*. Honolulu: University of Hawai'i Press.

—— 1999. *Ura: A Disappearing Language of Southern Vanuatu*. Canberra: Pacific Linguistics.

—— 2000. *An Erromangan (Sye) Dictionary*. Canberra: Pacific Linguistics.

—— 2002. 'Vinmavis'. In John Lynch, Malcolm Ross, and Terry Crowley, *The Oceanic Languages*, 638–49. London: Curzon Press.

CRYSTAL, DAVID. 2000. *Language Death*. Cambridge: Cambridge University Press.

DEACON, A. B. 1934 [1970]. *Malekula: A Vanishing People in the New Hebrides*, ed. Camilla H. Wedgwood. Oosterhout: Anthropological Publications.

DIMMENDAAL, GERRIT J. 2001. 'Places and people: field sites and informants'. In Paul Newman and Martha Ratliff (eds.), *Linguistic Fieldwork*, 55–75. Cambridge: Cambridge University Press.

DIXON, R. M. W. 1997. *The Rise and Fall of Languages*. Cambridge: Cambridge University Press.

—— 2001. 'A program for linguists'. Unpublished paper presented at the Fifteenth International Conference in Historical Linguistics. La Trobe University, Melbourne, 13–17 August 2001.

DONALDSON, TAMSIN. 1980. *Ngiyambaa: The Language of the Wangaaybuwan of New South Wales*. Cambridge: Cambridge University Press.

DORIAN, NANCY C. 2001. 'Surprises in Sutherland: linguistic variability amidst social uniformity'. In Paul Newman and Martha Ratliff (eds.), *Linguistic Fieldwork*, 133–51. Cambridge: Cambridge University Press.

DURANTI, ALESSANDRO. 1994. *From Grammar to Politics: Linguistic Anthropology in a Western Samoan Village*. Berkeley and Los Angeles: University of California Press.

—— 1997. *Linguistic Anthropology*. Cambridge: Cambridge University Press.

DWYER, ARIENNE. 2006. 'Ethics and practicalities of cooperative fieldwork and analysis'. In Jost Gippert, Nikolaus P. Himmelmann, and Ulrike Mosel. (eds.), *Essentials of Language Documentation*, 31–66. Berlin: Mouton De Gruyter.

EADES, DIANA. 1979. *The Dharawal and Dhurga languages of the New South Wales South Coast*. Canberra: Australian Institute of Aboriginal Studies.

EVANS, NICHOLAS. 2001. 'The last speaker is dead—long live the last speaker!' In Paul Newman and Martha Ratliff (eds.), *Linguistic Fieldwork*, 250–81. Cambridge: Cambridge University Press.

EVERETT, DANIEL L. 2001. 'Monolingual field research'. In Paul Newman and Martha Ratliff (eds.), *Linguistic Fieldwork*, 166–88. Cambridge: Cambridge University Press.

FARACLAS, NICHOLAS. 1996. 'New developments in literacy in Papua New Guinea languages'. In John Lynch and Fa'afo Pat (eds.), *Oceanic Studies: Proceedings of the First International Conference on Oceanic Linguistics*, 353–65. Canberra: Pacific Linguistics.

FOLEY, WILLIAM A. (ed.). 1993. *The Role of Theory in Language Description*. Berlin: Mouton de Gruyter.

FREEMAN, DEREK. 1983. *Margaret Mead and Samoa: The Making and Unmaking of an Anthropological Myth*. Cambridge, Mass.: Harvard University Press.

GARDINER, MARGARET. 1984. *Footprints on Malekula: A Memoir of Bernard Deacon*. Edinburgh: Salamander Press.

GERDTS, DONNA B. 1998. 'Beyond expertise: the role of the linguist in language revitalization'. In Nicholas Ostler (ed.), *Endangered languages: What Role for the Specialist?*, 13–22. Bath: The Foundation for Endangered Languages.

GIL, DAVID. 2001. 'Escaping Eurocentrism: fieldwork as a process of unlearning'. In Paul Newman and Martha Ratliff (eds.), *Linguistic Fieldwork*, 102–32. Cambridge: Cambridge University Press.

GREENBERG, JOSEPH H. 1966. 'Some universals of grammar with particular reference to the order of meaningful elements'. In Joseph H. Greenberg (ed.), *Universals of Language*, 2nd edn., 73–113. Cambridge, Mass.: The MIT Press.

—— 1971. 'The Indo-Pacific hypothesis'. In Thomas A. Sebeok (ed.), *Current Trends in Linguistics* (Vol. 8 of Linguistics in Oceania), 807–71. The Hague: Mouton.

HALE, KEN. 2001. 'Ulwa (Southern Sumu): the beginnings of a language research project'. In Paul Newman and Martha Ratliff (eds.), *Linguistic Fieldwork*, 76–101. Cambridge: Cambridge University Press.

HERCUS, LUISE. 1969. *The Languages of Victoria: A Late Survey* (Parts 1 and 2). Canberra: Australian Institute of Aboriginal Studies.

HIMMELMANN, NIKOLAUS P. 1998. 'Documentary and descriptive linguistics'. *Linguistics*, 36: 161–95.

HOLMES, LOWELL D. 1987. *The Quest for the Real Samoa: The Mead/Freeman Controversy and Beyond*. South Hadley, Mass.: Bergin and Garvey Publishers, Inc.

HYMAN, LARRY M. 2001. 'Fieldwork as a state of mind'. In Paul Newman and Martha Ratliff (eds.), *Linguistic Fieldwork*, 15–33. Cambridge: Cambridge University Press.

KAPLAN, ROBERT B., and RICHARD B. BALDAUF Jr. 2002. *Language and Language-in-Education Planning in the Pacific Basin*. Dordrecht: Kluwer.

KEESING, ROGER. 1975. *Kwaio Dictionary*. Canberra: Pacific Linguistics.

KING, MICHAEL. 2003. *The Penguin History of New Zealand*. Auckland: Penguin Books.

KRAUSS, MICHAEL. 1992. 'The world's languages in crisis'. *Language*, 68: 4–10.

KULICK, DON. 1995. 'The sexual life of anthropologists: erotic subjectivity and ethnographic work'. In Don Kulick and Margaret Willson (eds.), *Taboo: Sex, Identity and Erotic Subjectivity in Anthropological Fieldwork*, 219–50. London: Routledge.

LABOV, WILLIAM. 1972. 'The logic of nonstandard English'. In Pier Paolo Giglioli (ed.), *Language and Social Context*, 179–215. Harmondsworth: Penguin Books Ltd.

LADEFOGED, PETER. 2003. *Phonetic Data Analysis: An Introduction to Fieldwork and Instrumental Techniques*. Malden, Mass.: Blackwell Publishing.

LANDAU, SIDNEY I. 1989. *Dictionaries: The Art and Craft of Lexicography*. Cambridge: Cambridge University Press.

LYNCH, JOHN. 1998. *Pacific Languages: An Introduction*. Honolulu: University of Hawai'i Press.

—— and TERRY CROWLEY. 2001. *Languages of Vanuatu: A New Survey and Bibliography*. Canberra: Pacific Linguistics.

McCONVELL, PATRICK., and NICHOLAS THIEBERGER. 2001, *State of Indigenous languages in Australia—2001*, Australia State of the Environment Second Technical Paper Series (Natural and Cultural Heritage), Department of the Environment and Heritage, Canberra.

MADDIESON, IAN. 2001. 'Phonetic fieldwork'. In Paul Newman and Martha Ratliff (eds.), *Linguistic Fieldwork*, 211–29. Cambridge: Cambridge University Press.

MALINOWSKI, BRONISLAW. 1929. *The Sexual Life of Savages*. New York: Harcourt, Brace and Company.

MEAD, MARGARET. 1939. 'Native languages as field-work tools'. *American Anthropologist* 41: 189–205.

MILROY, LESLEY. 1987. *Observing and Analysing Natural Language: A Critical Account of Sociolinguistic Method*. Oxford: Oxford University Press.

MITHUN, MARIANNE. 2001. 'Who shapes the record: the speaker and the linguist'. In Paul Newman and Martha Ratliff (eds.), *Linguistic Fieldwork*, 34–54. Cambridge: Cambridge University Press.

MORENO, EVA. 1995. 'Rape in the field: reflections from a survivor'. In Don Kulick and Margaret Wilson (eds.), *Taboo: Sex, Identity and Erotic Subjectivity in Anthropological Fieldwork*, 219–50. London: Routledge.

MOSEL, ULRIKE, and EVEN HOVDHAUGEN. 1992. *Samoan Reference Grammar*. Oslo: Scandinavian University Press.

NETTLE, DANIEL, and SUZANNE ROMAINE. 2000. *Vanishing Voices: The Extinction of the World's Languages*. Oxford: Oxford University Press.

NEWMAN, PAUL, and MARTHA RATLIFF. 2001. 'Introduction'. In Paul Newman and Martha Ratliff (eds.), *Linguistic Fieldwork*, 1–14. Cambridge: Cambridge University Press.

OBEYESEKERE, GANARATH. 1992. *The Apotheosis of Captain Cook: European Mythmaking in the Pacific*. Princeton: Princeton University Press.

OKRAND, MARC. 1992. *The Klingon Dictionary: English/Klingon, Klingon/English*. New York: Pocket Books.

OSTLER, NICHOLAS. 1998. 'What role for the specialist?' In Nicholas Ostler (ed.), *Endangered Languages: What Role for the Specialist?*, 11–12. Bath: The Foundation for Endangered Languages.

PAYNE, THOMAS E. 1997. *Describing Morphosyntax: A Guide for Field Linguists*. Cambridge: Cambridge University Press.

RAE-ELLIS, VIVIENNE. 1981. *Trucanini: Queen or Traitor?* Canberra: Australian Institute of Aboriginal Studies.

—— 1988. *Black Robinson: Protector of Aborigines*. Melbourne: Melbourne University Press.

RICE, KEREN. 2001. 'Learning as one goes'. In Paul Newman and Martha Ratliff (eds.), *Linguistic Fieldwork*, 230–49. Cambridge: Cambridge University Press.

—— 2005. 'The linguist's responsibilities to the community of speakers'. Conference on Language Documentation: Theory, Practice, and Values. LSA Linguistic Institute, 9–10 July 2005.

—— to appear. 'Ethical issues in linguistic fieldwork: an overview'. To appear in W. van den Hoonaard (ed.), *The Ethics Trapeze*. Vancouver: University of British Columbia Press.

RYAN, LYNDALL. 1996. *The Aboriginal Tasmanians*, 2nd edn. Crows Nest (NSW): Allen & Unwin.

SAMARIN, WILLIAM J. 1967. *Field Linguistics: A Guide to Linguistic Field Work*. New York: Holt, Rinehart & Winston.

SCHIEFFELIN, BAMBI B., and ELINOR OCHS (eds.). 1986. *Language Socialization across Cultures*. Cambridge: Cambridge University Press.

SHOPEN, TIMOTHY (ed.) 1985a. *Language Typology and Syntactic Description*, i: *Clause Structure*. Cambridge: Cambridge University Press.

—— (ed.) 1985b. *Language Typology and Syntactic Description*, ii: *Complex Constructions*. Cambridge: Cambridge University Press.

—— (ed.) 1985c. *Language Typology and Syntactic Description*, iii: *Grammatical Categories and the Lexicon*. Cambridge: Cambridge University Press.

SUTTON, PETER, and MICHAEL WALSH. 1979. *Revised Linguistic Fieldwork Manual for Australia*. Canberra: Australian Institute of Aboriginal Studies.

THIEBERGER, NICHOLAS. 2004. 'Topics in the grammar and documentation of South Efate, an Oceanic language of Central Vanuatu'. Ph.D. dissertation, University of Melbourne.

VAUX, BERT., and JUSTIN COOPER. 1999. *Introduction to Linguistic Field Methods.* Munich: Lincom.

WHALEY, LINDAY J. 1997. *Introduction to Typology: The Unity and Diversity of Language.* Thousand Oaks, Calif.: SAGE Publications.

WILLIAMS, C. J. 1980. *A Grammar of Yuwaalaraay.* Canberra: Pacific Linguistics.

Index